# DB2 11 for z/OS:

# SQL Basic Training for Application Developers

Robert Wingate

ISBN 13: 9781797423159

**Disclaimer**

The contents of this book are based upon the author's understanding of and experience with the IBM DB2 product. Every attempt has been made to provide correct information. However, the author and publisher do not guarantee the accuracy of every detail, nor do they assume responsibility for information included in or omitted from it. All of the information in this book should be used at your own risk.

**Copyright**

# Contents

# Introduction

Congratulations on your purchase of **DB2 11 for z/OS: SQL Basic Training for Application Developers**! This book will teach you the basic information and skills you need to develop applications with DB2 SQL on IBM mainframe computers running z/OS. The instruction, examples and sample programs in this book are a fast track to becoming productive as quickly as possible using DB2 SQL. The content is easy to read and digest, well organized and focused on honing real job skills.

Thanks for your purchase and if you find this SQL basic training guide useful, please leave a positive review at the place you purchased it. I'll really appreciate that.

Best of luck with your DB2 career!

Robert Wingate
IBM Certified Application Developer – DB2 11 for z/OS

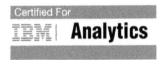

# Data Manipulation Language Basics

## Overview

Data Manipulation Language (DML) is used to add, change and delete data in a DB2 table. DML is one of the most basic and essential skills you must have as a DB2 professional. In this section we'll look at the five major DML statements: INSERT, UPDATE, DELETE, MERGE and SELECT. [1]

### Database, Tablespace and Schema Conventions

Throughout this book we will be using a database called DBHR which is for a fictitious human relations department in a company. The main tablespace we will use is TSHR. Finally, our default schema will be HRSCHEMA. In some cases we will explicitly specify the schema in our DDL or SQL. If we don't explicitly specify a schema, it means we have defined the HRSCHEMA schema as the CURRENT SCHEMA so we don't need to specify it.

If you are following along and creating examples on your own system, you may of course use whatever database and schema is available to you on your system. If you want the basic DDL to create the objects named above, it is as follows:

```
CREATE DATABASE DBHR
STOGROUP SGHR
BUFFERPOOL BPHR
INDEXBP IBPHR
CCSID UNICODE;

CREATE TABLESPACE TSHR
     IN DBHR
     USING STOGROUP SGHR
       PRIQTY 50
       SECQTY 20
     LOCKSIZE PAGE
     BUFFERPOOL BPHR2;

CREATE SCHEMA HRSCHEMA
AUTHORIZATION USER001;     ← This should be your DB2 id, whatever it is.
```

## DML SQL Statements

Data Manipulation Language (DML) is at the core of working with relational databases. You need to be very comfortable with DML statements: INSERT, UPDATE, DELETE, MERGE and SELECT. We'll cover the syntax and use of each of these. For purposes of this

---

[1] I realize that some sources do not consider the SELECT verb to be DML because it does not change the data. However I include it because it does in fact manipulate data by retrieving and displaying it. Also, you won't get far working with SQL without knowing the SELECT statement. So we cover it.

section, let's plan and create a very simple table. Here are the columns and data types for our table which we will name EMPLOYEE.

| Field Name | Type | Attributes |
|---|---|---|
| EMP_ID | INTEGER | NOT NULL, PRIMARY KEY |
| EMP_LAST_NAME | VARCHAR(30) | NOT NULL |
| EMP_FIRST_NAME | VARCHAR(20) | NOT NULL |
| EMP_SERVICE_YEARS | INTEGER | NOT NULL, DEFAULT IS ZERO |
| EMP_PROMOTION_DATE | DATE | |

The table can be created with the following DDL:

```
CREATE TABLE HRSCHEMA.EMPLOYEE(
EMP_ID INT NOT NULL,
EMP_LAST_NAME VARCHAR(30) NOT NULL,
EMP_FIRST_NAME VARCHAR(20) NOT NULL,
EMP_SERVICE_YEARS INT NOT NULL WITH DEFAULT 0,
EMP_PROMOTION_DATE DATE,
PRIMARY KEY(EMP_ID)) ;
```

We also need to create a unique index to support the primary key:

```
CREATE UNIQUE INDEX NDX_EMPLOYEE
ON EMPLOYEE (EMP_ID);
```

## INSERT Statement

The INSERT statement adds one or more rows to a table. There are three forms of the INSERT statement and you need to know the syntax of each of these.

1. Insert via Values

2. Insert via Select

3. Insert via FOR N ROWS

### Insert Via Values

There are actually two sub-forms of the insert by values. One form explicitly names the target columns and the other does not. Generally when inserting a record you explicitly specify the target columns, followed by a VALUES clause that includes the actual data values to apply to the new record. Let's use our EMPLOYEE table for this example:

```
INSERT INTO EMPLOYEE
(EMP_ID,
 EMP_LAST_NAME,
```

```
 EMP_FIRST_NAME,
 EMP_SERVICE_YEARS,
 EMP_PROMOTION_DATE)

VALUES (3217,
'JOHNSON',
'EDWARD',
4,
'01/01/2017')
```

Note that the specified values must be ordered in the same sequence that the columns are named in the query.

A second sub-form of the INSERT statement via values is to omit specifying the target fields and simply provide the VALUES clause. You can do this only if your values clause includes values for ALL the columns in the correct positional order as defined in the table.

Here's an example of this second sub-form of insert via values:

```
INSERT INTO EMPLOYEE
VALUES (7459,
'STEWART',
'BETTY',
7,
'07/31/2016')
```

Note that EMP_ID is defined as a primary key on the table. If you try inserting a row for which the primary key already exists, you will receive a -803 error SQL code.
Here's an example of specifying the DEFAULT value for the EMP_SERVICE_YEARS column, and the NULL value for the EMP_PROMOTION_DATE.

```
INSERT INTO EMPLOYEE
(EMP_ID,
EMP_LAST_NAME,
EMP_FIRST_NAME,
EMP_SERVICE_YEARS,
EMP_PROMOTION_DATE)

VALUES (9134,
'FRANKLIN',
'ROSEMARY',
DEFAULT,
NULL);
```

When you define a column using WITH DEFAULT, you do not necessarily have to specify the actual default value in your DDL. DB2 provides implicit default values for most data types and if you just specify WITH DEFAULT and no specific value, the implicit default value will be used.

In the EMPLOYEE table we specified WITH DEFAULT 0 for the employee's service years. However, the implicit default value is also zero because the column is defined as INTEGER. So we could have simply specified WITH DEFAULT and it would have the same result as specifying WITH DEFAULT 0.

The following table denotes the default values for the various data types.

| For columns of | Type | Default |
|---|---|---|
| Numbers | SMALLINT, INTEGER, BIGINT, DECIMAL, NUMERIC, REAL, DOUBLE, DECFLOAT, or FLOAT | 0 |
| Fixed-length strings | CHAR or GRAPHIC<br>BINARY | Blanks<br>Hexadecimal zeros |
| Varying-length strings | VARCHAR, CLOB, VARGRAPHIC, DBCLOB, VARBINARY, or BLOB | Empty string |
| Dates | DATE | CURRENT DATE |
| Times | TIME | CURRENT TIME |
| Timestamps | TIMESTAMP | CURRENT TIMESTAMP |
| ROWIDs | ROWID | DB2-generated |

Before moving on to the Insert via Select option, let's take a look at the data we have in the table so far.

```
SELECT EMP_ID,
EMP_LAST_NAME,
EMP_FIRST_NAME,
EMP_SERVICE_YEARS,
EMP_PROMOTION_DATE
FROM EMPLOYEE
ORDER BY EMP_ID;
-------+---------+---------+---------+---------+---------+---------+---------+-
   EMP_ID  EMP_LAST_NAME   EMP_FIRST_NAME   EMP_SERVICE_YEARS  EMP_PROMOTION_DATE
-------+---------+---------+---------+---------+---------+---------+---------+-
     3217  JOHNSON         EDWARD                          4   2017-01-01
     7459  STEWART         BETTY                           7   2016-01-01
     9134  FRANKLIN        ROSEMARY                        0   ----------

DSNE610I NUMBER OF ROWS DISPLAYED IS 3
```

**Insert via Select**

You can use a SELECT query to extract data from one table and load it to another. You can even include literals or built in functions in the SELECT query in lieu of column names (if you need them). Let's do an example.

Suppose you work in HR and you have an employee recognition request table named EMPRECOG. This table is used to generate/store recognition requests for employees who have been promoted during a certain time frame. Once the request is fulfilled, the date completed will be populated by HR in a separate process. The table specification is as follows:

| Field Name | Type | Attributes |
|---|---|---|
| EMP_ID | INTEGER | NOT NULL |
| EMP_PROMOTION_DATE | DATE | NOT NULL |
| EMP_RECOG_RQST_DATE | DATE | NOT NULL WITH DEFAULT |
| EMP_RECOG_COMP_DATE | DATE | |

The DDL to create the table is as follows:

```
CREATE TABLE EMPRECOG(
EMP_ID INT NOT NULL,
EMP_PROMOTION_DATE DATE NOT NULL,
EMP_RECOG_RQST_DATE DATE
NOT NULL WITH DEFAULT,
EMP_RECOG_COMP_DATE DATE)
IN TSHR;
```

Your objective is to load this table with data from the EMPLOYEE table for any employee whose promotion date occurs during the current month. The selection criteria could be expressed as:

```
SELECT
EMP_ID,
EMP_PROMOTION_DATE
FROM EMPLOYEE
WHERE MONTH(EMP_PROMOTION_DATE)
 = MONTH(CURRENT DATE)
```

To use this SQL in an INSERT statement on the EMPRECOG table, you would need to add another column for the request date (EMP_RECOG_RQST_DATE). Let's use the CURRENT DATE function to insert today's date. Now our select statement looks like this:

```
SELECT
EMP_ID,
EMP_PROMOTION_DATE,
```

```
CURRENT DATE AS RQST_DATE
FROM EMPLOYEE
WHERE MONTH(EMP_PROMOTION_DATE)
    = MONTH(CURRENT DATE)
```

Assuming we are running the SQL on January 10, 2017 we should get the following results:

```
---------+---------+---------+---------+---------+
    EMP_ID   EMP_PROMOTION_DATE   RQST_DATE
---------+---------+---------+---------+---------+
      3217   2017-01-01          2017-01-10

DSNE610I NUMBER OF ROWS DISPLAYED IS 1
```

Finally, let's create the actual INSERT statement for the EMPRECOG table. Since our query does not include the EMP_RQST_COMP_DATE (assume that the **request complete** column will be populated by another HR process when the request is complete), we must specify the target column names we are populating. Otherwise we will get a mismatch between the number of columns we are loading and the number in the table.

**Professional Note:** in circumstances where you have values for all the table's columns, you don't have to include the column names. You could just use the INSERT INTO and SELECT statement. But it is handy to include the target column names, even when you don't have to. It makes the DML more self-documenting and helpful for the next developer. This is a good habit to develop – thinking of the next person that will maintain your code.

Here is our SQL:

```
INSERT INTO EMPRECOG
(EMP_ID,
 EMP_PROMOTION_DATE,
 EMP_RECOG_RQST_DATE)
 SELECT
 EMP_ID,
 EMP_PROMOTION_DATE,
 CURRENT DATE AS RQST_DATE
 FROM EMPLOYEE
 WHERE MONTH(EMP_PROMOTION_DATE)
  = MONTH(CURRENT DATE)
```

If you are following along and running the examples, you may notice it doesn't work if the real date is not a January 2017 date. You can make this one work by specifying the comparison date as 01/01/2017 instead of the current date. So your query would be:

```
INSERT INTO EMPRECOG
(EMP_ID,
 EMP_PROMOTION_DATE,
 EMP_RECOG_RQST_DATE)
 SELECT
 EMP_ID,
 EMP_PROMOTION_DATE,
 CURRENT DATE AS RQST_DATE
 FROM EMPLOYEE
 WHERE MONTH(EMP_PROMOTION_DATE)
  = MONTH('01/01/2017');
```

After you run the SQL, query the EMPRECOG table, and you can see the result:

```
 SELECT * FROM EMPRECOG;
---------+---------+---------+---------+---------+---------+---------+---
    EMP_ID  EMP_PROMOTION_DATE  EMP_RECOG_RQST_DATE  EMP_RECOG_COMP_DATE
---------+---------+---------+---------+---------+---------+---------+---
     3217  2017-01-01            2017-01-10           ------------------
DSNE610I NUMBER OF ROWS DISPLAYED IS 1
```

The above is what we expect. Only one of the employees has a promotion date in January, 2017. This employee has been added to the EMPRECOG table with request date of January 10 and a NULL recognition completed date.

**Insert via FOR N ROWS**

The third form of the INSERT statement is used to insert multiple rows with a single statement. You can do this with an internal program table and host variables. We haven't talked yet about embedded SQL but we'll do a sample program now in COBOL along with a version in PLI, and I'll assume you know either the COBOL or PLI language. If you don't have compile JCL for your shop, check with your manager or technical leader to obtain it.

Before writing the program you will need to run a DCLGEN for the COBOL output structures. DCLGEN is an IBM utility that generates SQL data structures (table definition and host variables) for a table or view. DCLGEN stores the structure in a PDS member and then the PDS member can be included in a PLI or COBOL program by issuing an EXEC SQL INCLUDE statement. Put another way, DCLGEN generates table declarations (hence the name DCLGEN).

To specify COBOL as the language on the DCLGEN you must set the programming language default on the DB2I Defaults panel to IBMCOB. The following page shows the DB2I panel to set the APPLICATIONS LANGUAGE value.

```
                         DB2I DEFAULTS PANEL 1
COMMAND ===>

Change defaults as desired:

  1  DB2 NAME ............. ===> DBAX        (Subsystem identifier)
  2  DB2 CONNECTION RETRIES ===> 0           (How many retries for DB2 connection)
  3  APPLICATION LANGUAGE   ===> IBMCOB      (ASM, C, CPP, IBMCOB, FORTRAN, PLI)
  4  LINES/PAGE OF LISTING  ===> 60          (A number from 5 to 999)
  5  MESSAGE LEVEL ........ ===> I           (Information, Warning, Error, Severe)
  6  SQL STRING DELIMITER   ===> DEFAULT     (DEFAULT, ' or ")
  7  DECIMAL POINT ........ ===> .           (. or ,)
  8  STOP IF RETURN CODE >= ===> 8           (Lowest terminating return code)
  9  NUMBER OF ROWS ....... ===> 20          (For ISPF Tables)
 10  AS USER               ===>              (Userid to associate with the trusted
                                              connection)




PRESS:  ENTER to process    END to cancel          HELP for more information
```

## Next go to the DCLGEN option from the DB2I menu:

```
                        DB2I PRIMARY OPTION MENU           SSID: DBAX
COMMAND ===>
Select one of the following DB2 functions and press ENTER.

  1  SPUFI               (Process SQL statements)
  2  DCLGEN              (Generate SQL and source language declarations)
  3  PROGRAM PREPARATION (Prepare a DB2 application program to run)
  4  PRECOMPILE          (Invoke DB2 precompiler)
  5  BIND/REBIND/FREE    (BIND, REBIND, or FREE plans or packages)
  6  RUN                 (RUN an SQL program)
  7  DB2 COMMANDS        (Issue DB2 commands)
  8  UTILITIES           (Invoke DB2 utilities)
  D  DB2I DEFAULTS       (Set global parameters)
  Q  QMF                 (Query Management Facility)
  X  EXIT                (Leave DB2I)




PRESS:                      END to exit     HELP for more information
```

Fill in the needed information as follows:

```
                          DCLGEN                        SSID: DBAX
===>

Enter table name for which declarations are required:
  1   SOURCE TABLE NAME ===> EMPLOYEE

  2   TABLE OWNER ..... ===> HRSCHEMA

  3   AT LOCATION ..... ===>                             (Optional)
Enter destination data set:          (Can be sequential or partitioned)
  4   DATA SET NAME ... ===> 'HRUSER.DCLGEN.COBOL(EMPLOYEE)'
  5   DATA SET PASSWORD ===>          (If password protected)
Enter options as desired:
  6   ACTION .......... ===> ADD      (ADD new or REPLACE old declaration)
  7   COLUMN LABEL .... ===> NO       (Enter YES for column label)
  8   STRUCTURE NAME .. ===>                             (Optional)
  9   FIELD NAME PREFIX ===>                             (Optional)
 10   DELIMIT DBCS .... ===> YES      (Enter YES to delimit DBCS identifiers)
 11   COLUMN SUFFIX ... ===> NO       (Enter YES to append column name)
 12   INDICATOR VARS .. ===> NO       (Enter YES for indicator variables)
 13   ADDITIONAL OPTIONS===> NO       (Enter YES to change additional options

PRESS: ENTER to process    END to exit     HELP for more information
```

Now press ENTER to run the DCLGEN on the EMPLOYEE table to create the COBOL structures. Next, you will receive a message indicating the DCLGEN has succeeded.☐

```
      DSNE905I EXECUTION COMPLETE, MEMBER EMPLOYEE ADDED
      ***
```

Now you can browse the PDS member EMPLOYEE to see the resulting structures. The first structure will declare the DB2 table definition, and the other structure will declare COBOL host variables that correspond to the table definition.

```
      ************************************************************
      * DCLGEN TABLE(HRSCHEMA.EMPLOYEE)                         *
      *        LIBRARY(HRUSER01.DCLGEN.COBOL(EMPLOYEE))         *
      *        ACTION(ADD)                                      *
      *        LANGUAGE(COBOL)                                  *
      *        QUOTE                                            *
      * ... IS THE DCLGEN COMMAND THAT MADE THE FOLLOWING STATEMENTS  *
      ************************************************************
            EXEC SQL DECLARE HRSCHEMA.EMPLOYEE TABLE
              ( EMP_ID                      INTEGER NOT NULL,
                EMP_LAST_NAME               VARCHAR(30) NOT NULL,
                EMP_FIRST_NAME              VARCHAR(20) NOT NULL,
                EMP_SERVICE_YEARS           INTEGER NOT NULL,
                EMP_PROMOTION_DATE          DATE
              ) END-EXEC.
      ************************************************************
      * COBOL DECLARATION FOR TABLE HRSCHEMA.EMPLOYEE           *
      ************************************************************
       01   DCLEMPLOYEE.
            10 EMP-ID              PIC S9(9) USAGE COMP.
            10 EMP-LAST-NAME.
```

```
        49 EMP-LAST-NAME-LEN
           PIC S9(4) USAGE COMP.
        49 EMP-LAST-NAME-TEXT
           PIC X(30).
     10 EMP-FIRST-NAME.
        49 EMP-FIRST-NAME-LEN
           PIC S9(4) USAGE COMP.
        49 EMP-FIRST-NAME-TEXT
           PIC X(20).
     10 EMP-SERVICE-YEARS    PIC S9(9) USAGE COMP.
     10 EMP-PROMOTION-DATE   PIC X(10).
**********************************************************************
```

Next we'll insert two new rows into our EMPLOYEE using the INSERT via FOR N ROWS. Note that we define our host variables with OCCURS 2 TIMES to create arrays, and then we load the arrays with data before we do the INSERT statement. Also notice the **FOR 2 ROWS** clause at the end of the SQL statement. Of course, you could have an array with more than two rows. Also the number of rows you insert using FOR X ROWS can be less than the actual array size.

```
        IDENTIFICATION DIVISION.
        PROGRAM-ID. COBEMP1.

       ********************************************************
       *        PROGRAM USING DB2 INSERT FOR MULTIPLE ROWS    *
       ********************************************************

        ENVIRONMENT DIVISION.
        DATA DIVISION.
        WORKING-STORAGE SECTION.

           EXEC SQL
             INCLUDE SQLCA
           END-EXEC.

           EXEC SQL
             INCLUDE EMPLOYEE
           END-EXEC.

           01 HV-EMP-VARIABLES.
           10   HV-ID             PIC S9(9) USAGE COMP OCCURS 2 TIMES.
           10   HV-LAST-NAME      PIC X(30) OCCURS 2 TIMES.
           10   HV-FIRST-NAME     PIC X(20) OCCURS 2 TIMES.
           10   HV-SERVICE-YEARS  PIC S9(9) USAGE COMP OCCURS 2 TIMES.
           10   HV-PROMOTION-DATE PIC X(10) OCCURS 2 TIMES.

        PROCEDURE DIVISION.

        MAIN-PARA.
           DISPLAY "SAMPLE COBOL PROGRAM: MULTIPLE ROW INSERT".
```

```
*    LOAD THE EMPLOYEE ARRAY

         MOVE +4720              TO HV-ID (1).
         MOVE 'SCHULTZ'          TO HV-LAST-NAME(1).
         MOVE 'TIM'              TO HV-FIRST-NAME(1).
         MOVE +9                 TO HV-SERVICE-YEARS(1).
         MOVE '01/01/2017'       TO HV-PROMOTION-DATE(1).

         MOVE +6288              TO HV-ID (2).
         MOVE 'WILLARD'          TO HV-LAST-NAME(2).
         MOVE 'JOE'              TO HV-FIRST-NAME(2).
         MOVE +6                 TO HV-SERVICE-YEARS(2).
         MOVE '01/01/2016'       TO HV-PROMOTION-DATE(2).

*    LOAD THE EMPLOYEE TABLE

         EXEC SQL
            INSERT INTO HRSCHEMA.EMPLOYEE
            (EMP_ID,
             EMP_LAST_NAME,
             EMP_FIRST_NAME,
             EMP_SERVICE_YEARS,
             EMP_PROMOTION_DATE)

            VALUES
            (:HV-ID,
             :HV-LAST-NAME,
             :HV-FIRST-NAME,
             :HV-SERVICE-YEARS,
             :HV-PROMOTION-DATE)

            FOR 2 ROWS

         END-EXEC.

         STOP RUN.
```

An additional option for the multiple row INSERT is to specify ATOMIC or NOT ATOMIC. Specifying ATOMIC means that if any of the row operations fails, any successful row operations are rolled back. It's all or nothing. This may be what you want, but that will depend on your program design and how you plan to handle any failed rows.

```
EXEC SQL
   INSERT INTO HRSCHEMA.EMPLOYEE
   (EMP_ID,
    EMP_LAST_NAME,
    EMP_FIRST_NAME,
    EMP_SERVICE_YEARS,
    EMP_PROMOTION_DATE)
```

```
VALUES
(:HV-ID,
 :HV-LAST-NAME,
 :HV-FIRST-NAME,
 :HV-SERVICE-YEARS,
 :HV-PROMOTION-DATE)

FOR 2 ROWS
ATOMIC

END-EXEC.
STOP RUN.
```

Now let's create a PLI program to demonstrate the same multiple row INSERT technique. If you ran the COBOL program and added the two new employees, go ahead and delete them before continuing (we'll be adding the same rows again with the PLI program).

Before compiling you will need to run a DCLGEN for the PLI output structures. To specify PLI you will need to change the programming language default on the DB2I Defaults panel (remember during setup we initially set the application language to IBMCOB to specify the COBOL language). Here's the panel to change the APPLICATIONS LANGUAGE to PLI.

```
                         DB2I DEFAULTS PANEL 1
COMMAND ===>


Change defaults as desired:

 1  DB2 NAME .............. ===> DBAX        (Subsystem identifier)
 2  DB2 CONNECTION RETRIES ===> 0           (How many retries for DB2 connection)
 3  APPLICATION LANGUAGE   ===> PLI         (ASM, C, CPP, IBMCOB, FORTRAN, PLI)
 4  LINES/PAGE OF LISTING  ===> 60          (A number from 5 to 999)
 5  MESSAGE LEVEL ........ ===> I           (Information, Warning, Error, Severe)
 6  SQL STRING DELIMITER   ===> DEFAULT     (DEFAULT, ' or ")
 7  DECIMAL POINT ........ ===> .           (. or ,)
 8  STOP IF RETURN CODE >= ===> 8           (Lowest terminating return code)
 9  NUMBER OF ROWS ....... ===> 20          (For ISPF Tables)
10  AS USER               ===>             (Userid to associate with the trusted
                                            connection)


PRESS:  ENTER to process    END to cancel          HELP for more information
```

Now press ENTER to run the DCLGEN on the EMPLOYEE table to create the PLI structures.

Finally, here is the PLI program code.

```
PLIEMP1: PROCEDURE OPTIONS(MAIN) REORDER;
 /********************************************************************
 * PROGRAM NAME :   PLIEMP1 - PERFORM MULTI ROW INSERT TO DB2 TABLE *
 *******************************************************************/

 /********************************************************************
  *                  W O R K I N G   S T O R A G E               *
  *******************************************************************/

        DCL 01  HV_ID(2)              FIXED BIN(31);
        DCL 01  HV_LAST_NAME(2)       CHAR(30);
        DCL 01  HV_FIRST_NAME(2)      CHAR(20);
        DCL 01  HV_SERVICE_YEARS(2)   FIXED BIN(31);
        DCL 01  HV_PROMOTION_DATE(2)  CHAR(10);

     DCL RET_SQL_CODE              FIXED BIN(31) INIT(0);
     DCL RET_SQL_CODE_PIC          PIC 'S999999999' INIT (0);

     EXEC SQL
       INCLUDE SQLCA;

     EXEC SQL
       INCLUDE EMPLOYEE;


 /********************************************************************
  *                  P R O G R A M   M A I N L I N E            *
  *******************************************************************/

    PUT SKIP LIST ('SAMPLE PLI PROGRAM: MULTIPLE ROW INSERT');

    /* LOAD THE EMPLOYEE ARRAY */

        HV_ID(1)              = +4720;
        HV_LAST_NAME(1)       = 'SCHULTZ';
        HV_FIRST_NAME(1)      = 'TIM';
        HV_SERVICE_YEARS(1)   = +9;
        HV_PROMOTION_DATE(1)  = '01/01/2017';

        HV_ID(2)              = +6288;
        HV_LAST_NAME(2)       = 'WILLARD';
        HV_FIRST_NAME(2)      = 'JOE';
        HV_SERVICE_YEARS(2)   = +6;
        HV_PROMOTION_DATE(2)  = '01/01/2016';


        EXEC SQL
          INSERT INTO HRSCHEMA.EMPLOYEE
```

```
         (EMP_ID,
          EMP_LAST_NAME,
          EMP_FIRST_NAME,
          EMP_SERVICE_YEARS,
          EMP_PROMOTION_DATE)

          VALUES
          (:HV_ID,
           :HV_LAST_NAME,
           :HV_FIRST_NAME,
           :HV_SERVICE_YEARS,
           :HV_PROMOTION_DATE)

          FOR 2 ROWS
          ATOMIC;

    IF SQLCODE = 0 THEN;
    ELSE
        DO;
           EXEC SQL
              GET DIAGNOSTICS CONDITION 1
                :RET_SQL_CODE  = DB2_RETURNED_SQLCODE;

           RET_SQL_CODE_PIC   = RET_SQL_CODE;
           PUT SKIP LIST (RET_SQL_CODE_PIC);
        END;

 END PLIEMP1;
```

After you've pre-compiled, compiled, link-edited and bound your program, run it and now let's check out table contents:

```
SELECT
EMP_ID,
EMP_LAST_NAME,
EMP_FIRST_NAME,
EMP_SERVICE_YEARS,
EMP_PROMOTION_DATE
FROM EMPLOYEE
WHERE EMP_ID IN (3217, 4720, 6288, 7459, 9134)
ORDER BY EMP_ID;
---------+---------+---------+---------+---------+---------+---------+---------
    EMP_ID  EMP_LAST_NAME   EMP_FIRST_NAME   EMP_SERVICE_YEARS   EMP_PROMOTION_DATE
---------+---------+---------+---------+---------+---------+---------+---------
      3217  JOHNSON         EDWARD                           4   2017-01-01
      4720  SCHULTZ         TIM                              9   2017-01-01
      6288  WILLARD         JOE                              6   2016-01-01
      7459  STEWART         BETTY                            7   2016-01-01
      9134  FRANKLIN        ROSEMARY                         0   ----------
DSNE610I NUMBER OF ROWS DISPLAYED IS 5
```

**Note:**  On the ATOMIC option, you have another choice which is to specify NOT ATOMIC CONTINUE ON SQLEXCEPTION.  In this case any successful row operations are still applied

24

to the table, and any unsuccessful ones are not. The unsuccessfully inserted rows are discarded. The key point here is that NOT ATOMIC means the unsuccessful inserts do not cause the entire query to fail. Make sure to remember this point!

**Note2**: You can also INSERT to an underlying table via a view. The syntax is exactly the same as for inserting to a table. This topic will be considered in a later chapter.

## UPDATE Statement

The UPDATE statement is pretty straightforward. It changes one or more records based on specified conditions. There are two forms of the UPDATE statement:

1. The Searched Update

2. The Positioned Update

## Searched Update

The searched update is performed on records that meet a certain search criteria using a WHERE clause. The basic form and syntax you need to know for the searched update is:

```
UPDATE <TABLENAME>
SET FIELDNAME = <VALUE>
WHERE <CONDITION>
```

For example, recall that we left the promotion date for employee 9134 with a NULL value. Now let's say we want to update the promotion date to October 1, 2016. We could use this SQL to do that:

```
UPDATE EMPLOYEE
SET EMP_PROMOTION_DATE = '10/01/2016'
WHERE EMP_ID = 9134;
```

If you have more than one column to update, you must use a comma to separate the column names. For example, let's update both the promotion date and the first name of the employee. We'll make the first name Brianna and the promotion date 10/1/2016.

```
UPDATE EMPLOYEE
SET EMP_PROMOTION_DATE = '10/01/2016',
    EMP_FIRST_NAME = 'BRIANNA'
WHERE EMP_ID = 9134;
```

Another sub-form of the UPDATE statement to be aware of is UPDATE without a WHERE clause. For example, to set the **EMP_RECOG_COMP_DATE** field to January 31, 2017 for every row in the EMPRECOG table, you could use this statement:

```
UPDATE EMPRECOG
SET EMP_RECOG_COMP_DATE = '01/31/2017';
```

Obviously you should be very careful using this form of UPDATE, as it will change every row in the table. This is normally not what you want, but it could be useful in cases where you need to initialize one or more columns for all rows of a relatively small table.

## Positioned Update

The positioned update is an update based on a cursor in an application program. Let's continue with our EMPLOYEE table examples by creating an update DB2 program that will generate a result set based on a cursor, and then it will update a set of records.

We need to specially set up test data for our example, so if you are following along, execute the following query:

```
UPDATE EMPLOYEE
SET EMP_LAST_NAME = LOWER(EMP_LAST_NAME)
WHERE
EMP_LAST_NAME IN ('JOHNSON', 'STEWART', 'FRANKLIN');
```

Now here is the current content of our EMPLOYEE table:

```
SELECT EMP_ID, EMP_LAST_NAME, EMP_FIRST_NAME
FROM EMPLOYEE
ORDER BY EMP_ID;
```

| EMP_ID | EMP_LAST_NAME | EMP_FIRST_NAME |
|--------|---------------|----------------|
| 3217 | johnson | EDWARD |
| 4720 | SCHULTZ | TIM |
| 6288 | WILLARD | JOE |
| 7459 | stewart | BETTY |
| 9134 | franklin | BRIANNA |

As you can see we have some last names that are in lower case. Further, assume that we have decided we want to store all last names in upper case. So we have to correct the lowercase data. We want to check all records in the EMPLOYEE table and if the last name is in lower case, we want to change it to upper case. We also want to report the name (both before and after correction) of the corrected records.

To accomplish our objective we'll define and open a cursor on the EMPLOYEE table. We can specify a WHERE clause that limits the result set to only those records where the

`EMP_LAST_NAME` contains lower case characters. After we find them, we will change the case and replace the records.

To code a solution, first we need to identify the rows that include lower case letters in `EMP_LAST_NAME`. We can do this using the DB2 UPPER function. We'll compare the current contents of `EMP_LAST_NAME` to the value of `UPPER(EMP_LAST_NAME)` and if the results are not identical, we know that the row in question has lower case characters and needs to be changed. Our result set will include all rows where these two values are not identical. So our SQL would be:

```
SELECT EMP_ID, EMP_LAST_NAME
FROM HRSCHEMA.EMPLOYEE
WHERE EMP_LAST_NAME <> UPPER(EMP_LAST_NAME);
```

Once our FETCH statement has loaded the last name value into the host variable `EMP-LAST-NAME`, we can use the COBOL UPPER-CASE function to convert it from lowercase to uppercase.

```
MOVE FUNCTION UPPER-CASE (EMP-LAST-NAME) TO EMP-LAST-NAME
```

With this approach in mind, we are now ready to write the complete COBOL program. We will define and open the cursor, cycle through the result set using FETCH, modify the data and then do the UPDATE action specifying the current record of the cursor. That is what is meant by a positioned update – the cursor is positioned on the record to be changed, hence you do not need to specify a more elaborate WHERE clause in the UPDATE. Only the **WHERE CURRENT OF <cursor name>** clause need be specified. Also we will include the `FOR UPDATE` clause in our cursor definition to tell DB2 that our intent is to update the data we retrieve.

The program code follows:

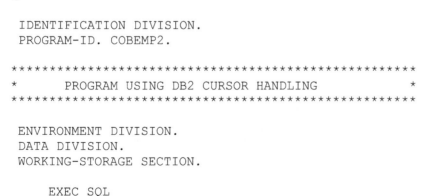

```
        IDENTIFICATION DIVISION.
        PROGRAM-ID. COBEMP2.

        **************************************************
        *       PROGRAM USING DB2 CURSOR HANDLING        *
        **************************************************

        ENVIRONMENT DIVISION.
        DATA DIVISION.
        WORKING-STORAGE SECTION.

            EXEC SQL
              INCLUDE SQLCA
            END-EXEC.
```

```
        EXEC SQL
          INCLUDE EMPLOYEE
        END-EXEC.

        EXEC SQL
            DECLARE EMP-CURSOR CURSOR FOR
            SELECT EMP_ID, EMP_LAST_NAME
            FROM EMPLOYEE
            WHERE EMP_LAST_NAME <> UPPER(EMP_LAST_NAME)
            FOR UPDATE OF EMP_LAST_NAME
        END-EXEC.


    PROCEDURE DIVISION.

    MAIN-PARA.
        DISPLAY "SAMPLE COBOL PROGRAM: UPDATE USING CURSOR".

        EXEC SQL
            OPEN EMP-CURSOR
        END-EXEC.

        DISPLAY 'OPEN CURSOR SQLCODE: ' SQLCODE.

        PERFORM FETCH-CURSOR
          UNTIL SQLCODE NOT EQUAL 0.

        EXEC SQL
            CLOSE EMP-CURSOR
        END-EXEC.

        DISPLAY 'CLOSE CURSOR SQLCODE: ' SQLCODE.

        STOP RUN.

    FETCH-CURSOR.

        EXEC SQL
            FETCH EMP-CURSOR INTO :EMP-ID, :EMP-LAST-NAME
        END-EXEC.

        IF SQLCODE = 0
            DISPLAY 'BEFORE CHANGE  ', EMP-LAST-NAME
            MOVE FUNCTION UPPER-CASE (EMP-LAST-NAME)
              TO EMP-LAST-NAME
            EXEC SQL
              UPDATE EMPLOYEE
              SET EMP_LAST_NAME = :EMP-LAST-NAME
              WHERE CURRENT OF EMP-CURSOR
```

28

```
          END-EXEC
       END-IF.

       IF SQLCODE = 0
          DISPLAY 'AFTER CHANGE   ', EMP-LAST-NAME
       END-IF.
```

Now it's necessary to compile and run the program. If you are following along and coding this program, I assume that you will pre-compile, compile, link-edit and bind your programs using whatever procedures are used in your shop.

After compiling and running, here is the output from running our COBOL program:

```
SAMPLE COBOL PROGRAM: UPDATE USING CURSOR
OPEN CURSOR SQLCODE: 0000000000
BEFORE CHANGE     johnson
AFTER CHANGE      JOHNSON
BEFORE CHANGE     stewart
AFTER CHANGE      STEWART
BEFORE CHANGE     franklin
AFTER CHANGE      FRANKLIN
CLOSE CURSOR SQLCODE: 0000000000
```

If you are using PLI, here is the PLI version of the program, and notice there is an UPPERCASE function in this language, too.

```
PLIEMP2: PROCEDURE OPTIONS(MAIN) REORDER;

 /******************************************************************
 * PROGRAM NAME :   PLIEMP2 - USE CURSOR TO UPDATE DB2 ROWS      *
 ******************************************************************/

 /******************************************************************
 *                  W O R K I N G   S T O R A G E               *
 ******************************************************************/

   DCL RET_SQL_CODE              FIXED BIN(31) INIT(0);
   DCL RET_SQL_CODE_PIC          PIC 'S999999999' INIT (0);


   EXEC SQL
     INCLUDE SQLCA;

   EXEC SQL
     INCLUDE EMPLOYEE;

   EXEC SQL
     DECLARE EMP_CURSOR CURSOR FOR
```

```
         SELECT EMP_ID, EMP_LAST_NAME
         FROM HRSCHEMA.EMPLOYEE
         WHERE EMP_LAST_NAME <> UPPER(EMP_LAST_NAME)
         FOR UPDATE OF EMP_LAST_NAME;


/*********************************************************************
/*                P R O G R A M    M A I N L I N E               *
*********************************************************************/

   PUT SKIP LIST ('SAMPLE PLI PROGRAM: CURSOR TO UPDATE ROWS');

   EXEC SQL OPEN EMP_CURSOR;

   PUT SKIP LIST ('OPEN CURSOR SQLCODE: ' || SQLCODE);

   IF SQLCODE = 0 THEN
      DO UNTIL (SQLCODE ¬= 0);
         CALL P0100_FETCH_CURSOR;
      END;

   EXEC SQL CLOSE EMP_CURSOR;

   PUT SKIP LIST ('CLOSE CURSOR SQLCODE: ' || SQLCODE);

   IF SQLCODE ¬= 0 THEN
      DO;
         EXEC SQL
            GET DIAGNOSTICS CONDITION 1
            :RET_SQL_CODE  = DB2_RETURNED_SQLCODE;

         RET_SQL_CODE_PIC  = RET_SQL_CODE;
         PUT SKIP LIST (RET_SQL_CODE_PIC);
      END;

P0100_FETCH_CURSOR: PROC;

   EXEC SQL
      FETCH EMP_CURSOR INTO :EMP_ID, :EMP_LAST_NAME;

   IF SQLCODE = 0 THEN
      DO;
         PUT SKIP LIST ('BEFORE CHANGE  ' || EMP_LAST_NAME);
         EMP_LAST_NAME = UPPERCASE(EMP_LAST_NAME);
         EXEC SQL
            UPDATE HRSCHEMA.EMPLOYEE
            SET EMP_LAST_NAME = :EMP_LAST_NAME
            WHERE CURRENT OF EMP_CURSOR;
         IF SQLCODE = 0 THEN
            PUT SKIP LIST ('AFTER CHANGE   ' || EMP_LAST_NAME);
```

```
      END;


  END P0100_FETCH_CURSOR;

  END PLIEMP2;
```

And here is the modified table:

```
SELECT * FROM EMPLOYEE
ORDER BY EMP_ID;
---------+---------+---------+---------+---------+---------+----
    EMP_ID  EMP_LAST_NAME               EMP_FIRST_NAME
---------+---------+---------+---------+---------+---------+----
     3217   JOHNSON                     EDWARD
     4720   SCHULTZ                     TIM
     6288   WILLARD                     JOE
     7459   STEWART                     BETTY
     9134   FRANKLIN                    BRIANNA
```

This method of using a positioned cursor update is something you will use often, particularly when you do not know your result set beforehand, and anytime you need to examine the content of the record before you perform the update.

## DELETE Statement

The DELETE statement is also pretty straightforward. It removes one or more records from the table based on specified conditions. As with the UPDATE statement, there are two forms of the DELETE statement:

1. The Searched Delete

2. The Positioned Delete

### Searched DELETE

The searched delete is performed on records that meet a certain criteria, i.e., based on a WHERE clause. The basic form and syntax you need to remember for the searched DELETE is:

```
DELETE FROM <TABLENAME>
WHERE <CONDITION>
```

For example, we might want to remove the record for the employee with id 9134. We could use this SQL to do that:

```
DELETE FROM EMPLOYEE WHERE EMP_ID = 9134;
```

Another sub-form of the DELETE statement to be aware of is the DELETE without a WHERE clause. For example, to remove all records from the EMPRECOG table, use this statement:

```
DELETE FROM EMPRECOG;
```

Be very careful using this form of DELETE, as it will remove every record from the target table. This is normally not what you want, but it could be useful in cases where you need to initialize a relatively small table to empty.

## Positioned Delete

The positioned DELETE is similar to the positioned UPDATE. It is a DELETE based on a cursor position in an application program. Let's create a DB2 program that will delete records based on a cursor. We'll have it delete any record where the employee has not received a promotion.

Before we can proceed, we need to add a record to the EMPLOYEE table because currently we have no records that lack a promotion date. So we will add one.

```
INSERT INTO EMPLOYEE
VALUES (1122, 'JENKINS', 'DEBORAH', 5, NULL);
```

At this time, we have a single record in the table for which the promotion data is NULL, which is employee 1122, Deborah Jenkins:

```
SELECT
EMP_ID,
EMP_LAST_NAME,
EMP_FIRST_NAME,
EMP_PROMOTION_DATE
FROM EMPLOYEE
ORDER BY EMP_ID;
```

```
---------+---------+---------+---------+---------+---------+---------+---
    EMP_ID  EMP_LAST_NAME     EMP_FIRST_NAME     EMP_PROMOTION_DATE
---------+---------+---------+---------+---------+---------+---------+---
      1122  JENKINS           DEBORAH            ----------
      3217  JOHNSON           EDWARD             2017-01-01
      4720  SCHULTZ           TIM                2017-01-01
      6288  WILLARD           JOE                2016-01-01
      7459  STEWART           BETTY              2016-07-31
DSNE610I NUMBER OF ROWS DISPLAYED IS 5
```

The SQL for our cursor should look like this:

```
SELECT
EMP_ID,
FROM EMPLOYEE
WHERE EMP_PROMOTION_DATE IS NULL
FOR UPDATE
```

We'll include the FOR UPDATE clause with our cursor to ensure DB2 knows our intention is to use the cursor to delete the records we retrieve. In case you are wondering, there is no FOR DELETE clause. The FOR UPDATE clause covers both updates and deletes.

Our program code will look like this:

```
        IDENTIFICATION DIVISION.
        PROGRAM-ID. COBEMP3.

        ****************************************************
        *       PROGRAM USING DB2 CURSOR HANDLING AND DELETE *
        ****************************************************

        ENVIRONMENT DIVISION.
        DATA DIVISION.
        WORKING-STORAGE SECTION.

            EXEC SQL
              INCLUDE SQLCA
            END-EXEC.

            EXEC SQL
              INCLUDE EMPLOYEE
            END-EXEC.

            EXEC SQL
                DECLARE EMP-CURSOR CURSOR FOR
                SELECT EMP_ID
                FROM HRSCHEMA.EMPLOYEE
                WHERE EMP_PROMOTION_DATE IS NULL
                FOR UPDATE
            END-EXEC.

        PROCEDURE DIVISION.

        MAIN-PARA.
            DISPLAY "SAMPLE COBOL PROGRAM: UPDATE USING CURSOR".

            EXEC SQL
                OPEN EMP-CURSOR
            END-EXEC.

            DISPLAY 'OPEN CURSOR SQLCODE: ' SQLCODE.
```

```
            PERFORM FETCH-CURSOR
              UNTIL SQLCODE NOT EQUAL 0.

            EXEC SQL
                CLOSE EMP-CURSOR
            END-EXEC.

            DISPLAY 'CLOSE CURSOR SQLCODE: ' SQLCODE.
            STOP RUN.

        FETCH-CURSOR.

            EXEC SQL
                FETCH EMP-CURSOR INTO :EMP-ID
            END-EXEC.

            IF SQLCODE = 0
              EXEC SQL
                DELETE HRSCHEMA.EMPLOYEE
                WHERE CURRENT OF EMP-CURSOR
              END-EXEC

            END-IF.
            IF SQLCODE = 0
              DISPLAY 'DELETED EMPLOYEE ', EMP-ID
            END-IF.
```

The output from the program looks like this:

```
SAMPLE COBOL PROGRAM: DELETE USING CURSOR
OPEN CURSOR SQLCODE: 0000000000
DELETED EMPLOYEE 000001122
CLOSE CURSOR SQLCODE: 0000000000
```

The PLI version of the program is as follows.

```
PLIEMP3: PROCEDURE OPTIONS(MAIN) REORDER;

  /******************************************************************
  * PROGRAM NAME :   PLIEMP3 - USE CURSOR TO DELETE DB2 ROWS       *
  ******************************************************************/

  /******************************************************************
  /*              W O R K I N G   S T O R A G E                    *
  ******************************************************************/

    DCL RET_SQL_CODE            FIXED BIN(31) INIT(0);
    DCL RET_SQL_CODE_PIC        PIC 'S999999999' INIT (0);
```

```
   EXEC SQL
     INCLUDE SQLCA;

   EXEC SQL
     INCLUDE EMPLOYEE;

   EXEC SQL
     DECLARE EMP_CURSOR CURSOR FOR
     SELECT EMP_ID
     FROM HRSCHEMA.EMPLOYEE
     WHERE EMP_PROMOTION_DATE IS NULL
     FOR UPDATE;

/*********************************************************************
*                 P R O G R A M   M A I N L I N E                  *
*********************************************************************/

   PUT SKIP LIST ('SAMPLE PLI PROGRAM: CURSOR TO DELETE ROWS');

   EXEC SQL OPEN EMP_CURSOR;

   PUT SKIP LIST ('OPEN CURSOR SQLCODE: ' || SQLCODE);

   IF SQLCODE = 0 THEN
      DO UNTIL (SQLCODE ¬= 0);
         CALL P0100_FETCH_CURSOR;
      END;

   EXEC SQL CLOSE EMP_CURSOR;

   PUT SKIP LIST ('CLOSE CURSOR SQLCODE: ' || SQLCODE);

   IF SQLCODE ¬= 0 THEN
      DO;
         EXEC SQL
            GET DIAGNOSTICS CONDITION 1
            :RET_SQL_CODE  = DB2_RETURNED_SQLCODE;

         RET_SQL_CODE_PIC  = RET_SQL_CODE;
         PUT SKIP LIST (RET_SQL_CODE_PIC);
      END;

P0100_FETCH_CURSOR: PROC;

   DCLEMPLOYEE = '';

   EXEC SQL
       FETCH EMP_CURSOR INTO :EMP_ID;
```

35

```
   IF SQLCODE = 0 THEN
      DO;
         EXEC SQL
            DELETE HRSCHEMA.EMPLOYEE
            WHERE CURRENT OF EMP_CURSOR;
         IF SQLCODE = 0 THEN
            PUT SKIP LIST ('DELETED EMPLOYEE ' || EMP_ID);
      END;


 END P0100_FETCH_CURSOR;

 END PLIEMP3;
```

A single row was deleted from the table, as we can confirm by querying EMPLOYEE:

```
SELECT EMP_ID,
EMP_PROMOTION_DATE
FROM HRSCHEMA.EMPLOYEE
ORDER BY EMP_ID;

---------+---------+---------+---------+---
    EMP_ID   EMP_PROMOTION_DATE
---------+---------+---------+---------+---
      3217  2017-01-01
      4720  2017-01-01
      6288  2016-01-01
      7459  2016-07-31
DSNE610I NUMBER OF ROWS DISPLAYED IS 4
```

As with the positioned update statement, the positioned delete is something you will use when you do not know your result set beforehand, or when you have to first examine the content of the record and then decide whether or not to delete it.

## MERGE Statement

The MERGE statement updates a target table or view using specified input data. Rows that already exist in the target table are updated as specified by the input source, and rows that do not exist in the target are inserted using data from that same input source.

So what problem does the merge solve? It adds/updates records for a table from a data source when you don't know beforehand whether the row already exists in the table or not. An example could be if you are updating data in your table based on a flat file you receive from another system, department or even another company. Assuming the other system does not send you an action code (add, change or delete), you won't know whether to use the INSERT or UPDATE statement.

One way of handling this situation is to first try doing an INSERT and if you get a -803 SQL error code, then you know the record already exists and cannot be inserted. In that case you would then need to do an UPDATE instead. Or you could first try doing an UPDATE and then if you received an SQLCODE +100, you would know the record does not exist and you would need to do an INSERT. This solution works, but it inevitably wastes some DB2 calls.

A more elegant solution is the MERGE statement. We'll look at an example of this below. You'll notice the example is a pretty long SQL statement, but don't be put off by that. The SQL is only slightly longer than the combined INSERT and UPDATE statements you would have needed to use otherwise.

### Single Row Merge Using Values

Let's go back to our EMPLOYEE table for this example. Let's say we have employee information for Deborah Jenkins whom we previously deleted, and now we want to apply her information back to the table. This information is being fed to us from another system which also supplied the EMP_ID, but let's assume we don't know whether that EMP_ID already exists in our EMPLOYEE table or not. So let's use the MERGE statement:

```
MERGE INTO EMPLOYEE AS T
USING
(VALUES (1122,
'JENKINS',
'DEBORAH',
5,
NULL))
AS S
(EMP_ID,
 EMP_LAST_NAME,
 EMP_FIRST_NAME,
 EMP_SERVICE_YEARS,
 EMP_PROMOTION_DATE)
ON S.EMP_ID = T.EMP_ID

WHEN MATCHED
   THEN UPDATE
      SET T.EMP_LAST_NAME      = S.EMP_LAST_NAME,
          T.EMP_FIRST_NAME     = S.EMP_FIRST_NAME,
          T.EMP_SERVICE_YEARS  = S.EMP_SERVICE_YEARS,
          T.EMP_PROMOTION_DATE = S.EMP_PROMOTION_DATE

WHEN NOT MATCHED
   THEN INSERT
      VALUES (S.EMP_ID,
      S.EMP_LAST_NAME,
```

```
        S.EMP_FIRST_NAME,
        S.EMP_SERVICE_YEARS,
        S.EMP_PROMOTION_DATE);
```

Note that the existing EMPLOYEE table is given with a T qualifier and the new information is given with S as the qualifier (these qualifier names are arbitrary – you can use anything you want). We are matching the new information to the table based on employee id. When the specified employee id is matched to an employee id on the table, an update is performed using the S values. If it is not matched to an existing record, then an insert is performed – again based on the S values.

To verify that our MERGE action was successful, let's take another look at our EMPLOYEE table.

```
SELECT
EMP_ID,
EMP_LAST_NAME,
EMP_FIRST_NAME,
EMP_PROMOTION_DATE
FROM EMPLOYEE
ORDER BY EMP_ID;

---------+---------+---------+---------+---------+---------+---------+---------+
    EMP_ID  EMP_LAST_NAME       EMP_FIRST_NAME      EMP_PROMOTION_DATE
---------+---------+---------+---------+---------+---------+---------+---------+
      1122  JENKINS             DEBORAH             ----------
      3217  JOHNSON             EDWARD              2017-01-01
      4720  SCHULTZ             TIM                 2017-01-01
      6288  WILLARD             JOE                 2016-01-01
      7459  STEWART             BETTY               2016-07-31
DSNE610I NUMBER OF ROWS DISPLAYED IS 5
```

## Merge Using HOST Variables

You can also do a merge in an application program using host variables. For this example, let's create a new table and a new program. The table will be EMP_PAY and it will include the base and bonus pay for each employee identified by employee id. Here are the columns we need to define.

| Field Name | Type | Attributes |
|---|---|---|
| EMP_ID | INTEGER | NOT NULL |
| EMP_REGULAR_PAY | DECIMAL | NOT NULL |
| EMP_BONUS | DECIMAL | |

The DDL looks like this:

```
CREATE TABLE EMP_PAY(
EMP_ID INT NOT NULL,
EMP_REGULAR_PAY DECIMAL (8,2) NOT NULL,
EMP_BONUS_PAY DECIMAL   (8,2));
```

Next, let's add a few records:

```
INSERT INTO HRSCHEMA.EMP_PAY
VALUES (3217, 80000.00, 4000);

INSERT INTO HRSCHEMA.EMP_PAY
VALUES (7459, 80000.00, 4000);

INSERT INTO HRSCHEMA.EMP_PAY
VALUES (9134, 70000.00, NULL);
```

Now the current data in the table is as follows:

```
SELECT * FROM EMP_PAY;
---------+---------+---------+---------+----
    EMP_ID  EMP_REGULAR_PAY  EMP_BONUS_PAY
---------+---------+---------+---------+----
      3217          80000.00        4000.00
      7459          80000.00        4000.00
      9134          70000.00   -------------
```

Ok, let's create an update file for the employees where some of the data is for brand new employees and some is for updating existing employees. We'll have the program read the file and use the input data with a MERGE statement to update the table. Here's the content of the file with the three fields, EMP_ID, EMP_REGULAR_PAY and EMP_BONUS_PAY:

```
----+----1----+----2----+----3---
3217    65000.00  5500.00
7459    85000.00  4500.00
9134    75000.00  2500.00
4720    80000.00  2500.00
6288    70000.00  2000.00
```

Looking at these records we know we will need to update three records that are already on the table, and we need to add two records that don't currently exist on the table.

Here is sample code for a MERGE program that is based on reading the above input file and applying the data to the EMP_PAY table. It differs from the single row insert example only in that we are using host variables for the update data rather than using hard coded values. The power of the MERGE statement should be getting clearer to you now.

```
        IDENTIFICATION DIVISION.
        PROGRAM-ID. COBEMP4.

    *****************************************************
    *       PROGRAM USING DB2 MERGE WITH HOST VARIABLES   *
    *****************************************************
```

```cobol
ENVIRONMENT DIVISION.
INPUT-OUTPUT SECTION.

    FILE-CONTROL.
        SELECT EMPLOYEE-FILE    ASSIGN TO EMPFILE.

DATA DIVISION.

FILE SECTION.
FD  EMPLOYEE-FILE
    RECORDING MODE IS F
    LABEL RECORDS ARE STANDARD
    RECORD CONTAINS 80 CHARACTERS
    BLOCK CONTAINS 0 RECORDS.

    01 EMPLOYEE-RECORD.
        05  E-ID           PIC X(04).
        05  FILLER         PIC X(76).


WORKING-STORAGE SECTION.

    EXEC SQL
      INCLUDE SQLCA
    END-EXEC.

    EXEC SQL
      INCLUDE EMPPAY
    END-EXEC.

    01 WS-FLAGS.
        05  SW-END-OF-FILE-SWITCH    PIC X(1) VALUE 'N'.
        88  SW-END-OF-FILE                    VALUE 'Y'.
        88  SW-NOT-END-OF-FILE                VALUE 'N'.

    01 IN-EMPLOYEE-RECORD.
        05  EMPLOYEE-ID    PIC X(04).
        05  FILLER         PIC X(05).
        05  REGULAR-PAY    PIC 99999.99.
        05  FILLER         PIC X(02).
        05  BONUS-PAY      PIC 9999.99.
        05  FILLER         PIC X(54).


PROCEDURE DIVISION.

MAIN-PARA.
    DISPLAY "SAMPLE COBOL PROGRAM: UPDATE USING MERGE".
```

```
      OPEN INPUT EMPLOYEE-FILE.

*   MAIN LOOP - READ THE INPUT FILE, LOAD HOST VARIABLES
*               AND CALL THE MERGE ROUTINE.

      PERFORM UNTIL SW-END-OF-FILE

          READ EMPLOYEE-FILE INTO IN-EMPLOYEE-RECORD
             AT END SET SW-END-OF-FILE TO TRUE
          END-READ

          IF SW-END-OF-FILE
             CLOSE EMPLOYEE-FILE
          ELSE
             MOVE EMPLOYEE-ID TO  EMP-ID
             MOVE REGULAR-PAY TO  EMP-REGULAR-PAY
             MOVE BONUS-PAY   TO  EMP-BONUS-PAY
             PERFORM A1000-MERGE-RECORD
          END-IF

      END-PERFORM.

      STOP RUN.

  A1000-MERGE-RECORD.

     EXEC SQL

         MERGE INTO EMP_PAY AS TARGET
         USING (VALUES(:EMP-ID,
         :EMP-REGULAR-PAY,
         :EMP-BONUS-PAY))
         AS SOURCE(EMP_ID,
         EMP_REGULAR_PAY,
         EMP_BONUS_PAY)
         ON TARGET.EMP_ID = SOURCE.EMP_ID

         WHEN MATCHED THEN UPDATE
            SET TARGET.EMP_REGULAR_PAY
                  = SOURCE.EMP_REGULAR_PAY,
                TARGET.EMP_BONUS_PAY
                  = SOURCE.EMP_BONUS_PAY

         WHEN NOT MATCHED THEN INSERT
           (EMP_ID,
            EMP_REGULAR_PAY,
            EMP_BONUS_PAY)
            VALUES
            (SOURCE.EMP_ID,
             SOURCE.EMP_REGULAR_PAY,
```

```
                    SOURCE.EMP_BONUS_PAY)

          END-EXEC.

          IF SQLCODE = 0
             DISPLAY 'RECORD MERGED SUCCESSFULLY', EMP-ID
          ELSE
             DISPLAY 'ERROR - SQLCODE = ', SQLCODE, EMP-ID
          END-IF.
```

Here are the results from running the program.

```
SAMPLE COBOL PROGRAM: UPDATE USING MERGE
RECORD MERGED SUCCESSFULLY   000003217
RECORD MERGED SUCCESSFULLY   000007459
RECORD MERGED SUCCESSFULLY   000009134
RECORD MERGED SUCCESSFULLY   000004720
RECORD MERGED SUCCESSFULLY   000006288
```

Finally, here is the PLI version of the program.

```
PLIEMP4: PROCEDURE OPTIONS(MAIN) REORDER;
 /****************************************************************
 * PROGRAM NAME :   PLIEMP4 - USE DB2 MERGE WITH HOST VARIABLES.   *
 ****************************************************************/

 /****************************************************************
 *                 F I L E S                                    *
 ****************************************************************/
    DCL EMPFILE   FILE RECORD SEQL INPUT;

 /****************************************************************
 *                 W O R K I N G   S T O R A G E                *
 ****************************************************************/

    DCL SW_END_OF_FILE           STATIC BIT(01) INIT('0'B);

    DCL 01 IN_EMPLOYEE_RECORD,
           05  EMPLOYEE_ID   CHAR(04),
           05  FILLER1       CHAR(05),
           05  REGULAR_PAY   PIC '99999V.99',
           05  FILLER2       CHAR(02),
           05  BONUS_PAY     PIC '9999V.99',
           05  FILLER3       CHAR(54);

    DCL EMP_REGULAR_PAY_FD  FIXED DEC (8,2);
    DCL EMP_BONUS_PAY_FD    FIXED DEC (8,2);
```

42

```
   DCL RET_SQL_CODE              FIXED BIN(31) INIT(0);
   DCL RET_SQL_CODE_PIC          PIC 'SZZZZZ9999' INIT (0);

   EXEC SQL
     INCLUDE SQLCA;

   EXEC SQL
     INCLUDE EMPPAY;


/*******************************************************************
/*              O N   C O N D I T I O N S                        *
*******************************************************************/

   ON ENDFILE (EMPFILE) SW_END_OF_FILE =  '1'B;

/*******************************************************************
/*             P R O G R A M   M A I N L I N E                   *
*******************************************************************/

   PUT SKIP LIST ('SAMPLE PLI PROGRAM: UPDATE USING MERGE');

        OPEN FILE(EMPFILE);

        READ FILE (EMPFILE) INTO (IN_EMPLOYEE_RECORD);

      /* MAIN LOOP - READ THE INPUT FILE, LOAD HOST VARIABLES  */
      /*             AND CALL THE MERGE ROUTINE.               */

        DO WHILE (¬SW_END_OF_FILE);

            EMP_ID              = EMPLOYEE_ID;
            EMP_REGULAR_PAY_FD = REGULAR_PAY;
            EMP_BONUS_PAY_FD   = BONUS_PAY;
            EMP_REGULAR_PAY    = EMP_REGULAR_PAY_FD;
            EMP_BONUS_PAY      = EMP_BONUS_PAY_FD;
            CALL A1000_MERGE_RECORD;
            READ FILE (EMPFILE) INTO (IN_EMPLOYEE_RECORD);

        END; /* DO WHILE */

        CLOSE FILE(EMPFILE);

   A1000_MERGE_RECORD: PROC;

        EXEC SQL

          MERGE INTO EMP_PAY AS TARGET
          USING (VALUES(:EMP_ID,
          :EMP_REGULAR_PAY,
```

```
                          :EMP_BONUS_PAY))
                          AS SOURCE(EMP_ID,
                          EMP_REGULAR_PAY,
                          EMP_BONUS_PAY)
                          ON TARGET.EMP_ID = SOURCE.EMP_ID

                          WHEN MATCHED THEN UPDATE
                             SET TARGET.EMP_REGULAR_PAY
                                    = SOURCE.EMP_REGULAR_PAY,
                                 TARGET.EMP_BONUS_PAY
                                    = SOURCE.EMP_BONUS_PAY

                          WHEN NOT MATCHED THEN INSERT

                            (EMP_ID,
                             EMP_REGULAR_PAY,
                             EMP_BONUS_PAY)
                             VALUES
                             (SOURCE.EMP_ID,
                              SOURCE.EMP_REGULAR_PAY,
                              SOURCE.EMP_BONUS_PAY);

                    IF SQLCODE = 0 THEN
                        PUT SKIP LIST ('RECORD MERGED SUCCESSFULLY ' || EMP_ID);
                    ELSE
                        DO;
                           PUT SKIP LIST ('*** SQL ERROR ***');
                           EXEC SQL
                              GET DIAGNOSTICS CONDITION 1
                               :RET_SQL_CODE   = DB2_RETURNED_SQLCODE;

                           RET_SQL_CODE_PIC   = RET_SQL_CODE;
                           PUT SKIP LIST (RET_SQL_CODE_PIC);
                        END;

              END A1000_MERGE_RECORD;

          END PLIEMP4;
```

And the output from the PLI version:

```
SAMPLE PLI PROGRAM: UPDATE USING MERGE
RECORD MERGED SUCCESSFULLY        3217
RECORD MERGED SUCCESSFULLY        7459
RECORD MERGED SUCCESSFULLY        9134
RECORD MERGED SUCCESSFULLY        4720
RECORD MERGED SUCCESSFULLY        6288
```

And now we can verify that the results were actually applied to the table.

```
SELECT *
from EMP_PAY;

---------+---------+---------+---------+-------
     EMP_ID  EMP_REGULAR_PAY  EMP_BONUS_PAY
---------+---------+---------+---------+-------
       3217         65000.00         5500.00
       7459         85000.00         4500.00
       9134         75000.00         2500.00
       4720         80000.00         2500.00
       6288         70000.00         2000.00
DSNE610I NUMBER OF ROWS DISPLAYED IS 5
```

Again the power of the MERGE statement is that you do not need to know whether a record already exists when you apply the data to the table. The program logic is simplified – there is no trial and error to determine whether or not the record exists.

## SELECT Statement

SELECT is the main statement you will use to retrieve data from a table or view. The basic syntax for the select statement is:

```
SELECT              <column names>
FROM                <table or view name>
WHERE               <condition>
ORDER BY      <column name or number to sort by>
```

Let's return to our EMPLOYEE table for an example:

```
SELECT EMP_ID, EMP_LAST_NAME, EMP_FIRST_NAME
FROM HRSCHEMA.EMPLOYEE
WHERE EMP_ID = 3217;

---------+---------+---------+---------+---------+-----
     EMP_ID  EMP_LAST_NAME        EMP_FIRST_NAME
---------+---------+---------+---------+---------+-----
       3217  JOHNSON                 EDWARD
DSNE610I NUMBER OF ROWS DISPLAYED IS 1
```

You can also change the column heading on the result set by specifying <column name> AS <literal>. For example:

```
SELECT EMP_ID AS "EMPLOYEE NUMBER",
EMP_LAST_NAME AS "EMPLOYEE LAST NAME",
EMP_FIRST_NAME AS "EMPLOYEE FIRST NAME"
FROM HRSCHEMA.EMPLOYEE WHERE EMP_ID = 3217 ;
---------+---------+---------+---------+---------+---------+---
```

```
EMPLOYEE NUMBER  EMPLOYEE LAST NAME    EMPLOYEE FIRST NAME
---------+---------+---------+---------+---------+---------+---
         3217  JOHNSON              EDWARD
DSNE610I NUMBER OF ROWS DISPLAYED IS 1
```

Now let's look at some clauses that will further qualify the rows that are returned.

## WHERE CONDITION

There are quite a lot of options for the WHERE condition. In fact, you can use multiple where conditions by specifying AND and OR clauses. Be aware of the equality operators which are:

| | |
|---|---|
| = | Equal to |
| <> | Not equal to |
| > | Greater than |
| >= | Greater than or equal to |
| < | Less than |
| <= | Less than or equal to |

Let's look at some various examples of WHERE conditions.

## OR

```
  SELECT EMP_ID, EMP_LAST_NAME, EMP_FIRST_NAME
  FROM EMPLOYEE
  WHERE EMP_ID = 3217 OR EMP_ID = 9134;
---------+---------+---------+---------+---------+---------
    EMP_ID  EMP_LAST_NAME       EMP_FIRST_NAME
---------+---------+---------+---------+---------+---------
      3217  JOHNSON             EDWARD
      9134  FRANKLIN            BRIANNA
DSNE610I NUMBER OF ROWS DISPLAYED IS 2
```

## AND

```
  SELECT EMP_ID,
  EMP_LAST_NAME,
  EMP_FIRST_NAME,
  EMP_PROMOTION_DATE
  FROM HRSCHEMA.EMPLOYEE
  WHERE (EMP_SERVICE_YEARS > 1)
    AND (EMP_PROMOTION_DATE > '12/31/2016')

---------+---------+---------+---------+---------+---------+---------+---
    EMP_ID  EMP_LAST_NAME       EMP_FIRST_NAME      EMP_PROMOTION_DATE
---------+---------+---------+---------+---------+---------+---------+---
      3217  JOHNSON             EDWARD              2017-01-01
      4720  SCHULTZ             TIM                 2017-01-01
DSNE610I NUMBER OF ROWS DISPLAYED IS 2
```

## IN

You can specify that the column value must be present in a specified collection of values, either those you code in the SQL explicitly or a collection that is a result of a query. Let's look at an example of specifying EMP_IDs.

```
SELECT EMP_ID,
EMP_LAST_NAME,
EMP_FIRST_NAME
FROM HRSCHEMA.EMPLOYEE
WHERE EMP_ID IN (3217, 9134);
---------+---------+---------+---------+---------+
    EMP_ID  EMP_LAST_NAME       EMP_FIRST_NAME
---------+---------+---------+---------+---------+
      3217  JOHNSON             EDWARD
      9134  FRANKLIN            BRIANNA
DSNE610I NUMBER OF ROWS DISPLAYED IS 2
```

Now let's provide a listing of employees who are in the EMPLOYEE table but are NOT in the EMP_PAY table yet. This example shows us two new techniques, use of the NOT keyword and use of a sub-select to create a collection result set. First, let's add a couple of records to the EMPLOYEE table:

```
INSERT INTO EMPLOYEE
(EMP_ID,
EMP_LAST_NAME,
EMP_FIRST_NAME,
EMP_SERVICE_YEARS,
EMP_PROMOTION_DATE)

VALUES (3333,
'FORD',
'JAMES',
7,
'10/01/2015');

INSERT INTO EMPLOYEE
(EMP_ID,
EMP_LAST_NAME,
EMP_FIRST_NAME,
EMP_SERVICE_YEARS,
EMP_PROMOTION_DATE)

VALUES (7777,
'HARRIS',
'ELISA',
2,
NULL);
```

Now let's run our mismatch query:

```
        SELECT EMP_ID,
        EMP_LAST_NAME,
        EMP_FIRST_NAME
        FROM EMPLOYEE
        WHERE EMP_ID
        NOT IN (SELECT EMP_ID FROM EMP_PAY);
---------+---------+---------+---------+---------+---------+-
    EMP_ID  EMP_LAST_NAME       EMP_FIRST_NAME
---------+---------+---------+---------+---------+---------+-
       3333   FORD                 JAMES
       7777   HARRIS               ELISA
DSNE610I NUMBER OF ROWS DISPLAYED IS 2
```

By the way you can also use the **EXCEPT** clause to identify rows in one table that have no counterpart in the other. For example, suppose we want the employee ids of any employee who has not received a paycheck. You could quickly identify them with this SQL:

```
        SELECT EMP_ID
        FROM EMPLOYEE
        EXCEPT (SELECT EMP_ID FROM EMP_PAY);
---------+---------+---------+---------+---------+---
    EMP_ID
---------+---------+---------+---------+---------+---
       3333
       7777
DSNE610I NUMBER OF ROWS DISPLAYED IS 2
```

One limitation of the EXCEPT clause is that the two queries have to match exactly, so you could not bring back a column from EMPLOYEE that does not also exist in the EMP_PAY table. Still the EXCEPT is useful in some cases, especially where you need to identify discrepancies between tables using a single column.

## BETWEEN

The BETWEEN clause allows you to specify a range of values inclusive of the start and end value you provide. Here's an example where we want to retrieve the employee id and pay rate for all employees whose pay rate is between 60,000 and 85,000 annually.

```
    SELECT EMP_ID,
    EMP_REGULAR_PAY
    FROM EMP_PAY
    WHERE EMP_REGULAR_PAY
    BETWEEN 60000 AND 85000;
```

```
---------+---------+---------+---------+----
    EMP_ID  EMP_REGULAR_PAY
---------+---------+---------+---------+----
     3217          65000.00
     7459          85000.00
     9134          75000.00
     4720          80000.00
     6288          70000.00
DSNE610I NUMBER OF ROWS DISPLAYED IS 5
```

## LIKE

You can use the LIKE predicate to select values that match a pattern. For example, let's choose all rows for which the last name begins with the letter B. The % character is used as a wild card for any string value or character. So in this case we are retrieving every record for which the EMP_FIRST_NAME starts with the letter B.

```
SELECT EMP_ID,
EMP_LAST_NAME,
EMP_FIRST_NAME
FROM HRSCHEMA.EMPLOYEE
WHERE EMP_FIRST_NAME LIKE 'B%'
---------+---------+---------+---------+---------+---------
    EMP_ID  EMP_LAST_NAME        EMP_FIRST_NAME
---------+---------+---------+---------+---------+---------
     7459  STEWART              BETTY
     9134  FRANKLIN             BRIANNA
DSNE610I NUMBER OF ROWS DISPLAYED IS 2
```

## DISTINCT

Use the DISTINCT operator when you want to eliminate duplicate values. To illustrate this, let's create a couple of new tables. The first is called EMP_PAY_CHECK and we will use to store a calculated bi-monthly pay amount for each employee based on their annual salary. The DDL to create EMP_PAY_CHECK is a s follows:

```
CREATE TABLE EMP_PAY_CHECK(
EMP_ID INT NOT NULL,
EMP_REGULAR_PAY  DECIMAL (8,2) NOT NULL,
EMP_SEMIMTH_PAY DECIMAL (8,2) NOT NULL)
IN TSHR;
```

Now let's insert data into EMP_PAY_CHECK by calculating a twice monthly pay check:

```
INSERT INTO EMP_PAY_CHECK
(SELECT EMP_ID,
EMP_REGULAR_PAY,
EMP_REGULAR_PAY / 24 FROM EMP_PAY);
```

Let's look at the results:

```
SELECT * FROM HRSCHEMA.EMP_PAY_CHECK;
---------+---------+---------+---------+---------+--
   EMP_ID  EMP_REGULAR_PAY  EMP_SEMIMTH_PAY
---------+---------+---------+---------+---------+--
     3217       65000.00         2708.33
     7459       85000.00         3541.66
     9134       75000.00         3125.00
     4720       80000.00         3333.33
     6288       70000.00         2916.66
```

We now know how much each employee should make in their pay check. The next step is to create a history table of each pay check the employee receives. First we'll create the table and then we'll load it with data.

```
CREATE TABLE EMP_PAY_HIST(
EMP_ID INT NOT NULL,
EMP_PAY_DATE  DATE NOT NULL,
EMP_PAY_AMT   DECIMAL (8,2) NOT NULL)
IN TSHR;
```

We can load the history table by creating pay checks for the first four pay periods of the year like this:

```
INSERT INTO EMP_PAY_HIST
SELECT EMP_ID,
 '01/15/2017',
 EMP_SEMIMTH_PAY
 FROM EMP_PAY_CHECK;

INSERT INTO EMP_PAY_HIST
SELECT EMP_ID,
 '01/31/2017',
 EMP_SEMIMTH_PAY
 FROM EMP_PAY_CHECK;

INSERT INTO EMP_PAY_HIST
SELECT EMP_ID,
 '02/15/2017',
 EMP_SEMIMTH_PAY
 FROM EMP_PAY_CHECK;

INSERT INTO EMP_PAY_HIST
SELECT EMP_ID,
 '02/28/2017',
 EMP_SEMIMTH_PAY
 FROM EMP_PAY_CHECK;
```

Now we can look at the history table content which is as follows:

```
SELECT * from HRSCHEMA.EMP_PAY_HIST;
---------+---------+---------+---------+------
    EMP_ID  EMP_PAY_DATE  EMP_PAY_AMT
---------+---------+---------+---------+------
      3217  2017-01-15        2708.33
      7459  2017-01-15        3541.66
      9134  2017-01-15        3125.00
      4720  2017-01-15        3333.33
      6288  2017-01-15        2916.66
      3217  2017-01-31        2708.33
      7459  2017-01-31        3541.66
      9134  2017-01-31        3125.00
      4720  2017-01-31        3333.33
      6288  2017-01-31        2916.66
      3217  2017-02-15        2708.33
      7459  2017-02-15        3541.66
      9134  2017-02-15        3125.00
      4720  2017-02-15        3333.33
      6288  2017-02-15        2916.66
      3217  2017-02-28        2708.33
      7459  2017-02-28        3541.66
      9134  2017-02-28        3125.00
      4720  2017-02-28        3333.33
      6288  2017-02-28        2916.66
DSNE610I NUMBER OF ROWS DISPLAYED IS 20
```

If you want a list of all employees who got a paycheck during the month of February, you would need to eliminate the duplicate entries because there are two for each employee. You could accomplish that with this SQL:

```
SELECT DISTINCT EMP_ID
FROM HRSCHEMA.EMP_PAY_HIST
WHERE MONTH(EMP_PAY_DATE) = '02';

---------+---------+---------+---------+-----
    EMP_ID
---------+---------+---------+---------+-----
      3217
      4720
      6288
      7459
      9134
DSNE610I NUMBER OF ROWS DISPLAYED IS 5
```

51

The DISTINCT operator ensures that only unique records are selected based on the columns you are returning. This is important because if you included additional columns in the results, any value that makes the record unique will also make it **NOT** a duplicate. Let's illustrate this by adding the payment date to our query and see the results:

```
SELECT DISTINCT EMP_ID, EMP_PAY_DATE
FROM HRSCHEMA.EMP_PAY_HIST
WHERE MONTH(EMP_PAY_DATE) = '02'

---------+---------+---------+---------+----
    EMP_ID  EMP_PAY_DATE
---------+---------+---------+---------+----
      3217  2017-02-15
      3217  2017-02-28
      4720  2017-02-15
      4720  2017-02-28
      6288  2017-02-15
      6288  2017-02-28
      7459  2017-02-15
      7459  2017-02-28
      9134  2017-02-15
      9134  2017-02-28
DSNE610I NUMBER OF ROWS DISPLAYED IS 10
```

Since the combination of the employee id and payment date makes each record unique, you'll get multiple rows for each employee. So you must be careful in using DISTINCT to ensure that the structure of your query is really what you want.

## FETCH FIRST X ROWS ONLY

You can limit your result set by using the FETCH FIRST X ROWS ONLY clause. For example, suppose you just want the employee id and names of the first four records from the employee table. You can code it as follows:

```
SELECT EMP_ID,
EMP_LAST_NAME,
EMP_FIRST_NAME
FROM HRSCHEMA.EMPLOYEE
FETCH FIRST 4 ROWS ONLY
---------+---------+---------+---------+---------+-
    EMP_ID  EMP_LAST_NAME        EMP_FIRST_NAME
---------+---------+---------+---------+---------+-
      3217  JOHNSON              EDWARD
      7459  STEWART              BETTY
      9134  FRANKLIN             BRIANNA
      4720  SCHULTZ              TIM
DSNE610I NUMBER OF ROWS DISPLAYED IS 4
```

Keep in mind that when you order the results you may get different records. For example if you order by last name, you would get this result:

```
SELECT EMP_ID,
EMP_LAST_NAME,
EMP_FIRST_NAME
FROM HRSCHEMA.EMPLOYEE
ORDER BY EMP_LAST_NAME
FETCH FIRST 4 ROWS ONLY
```

```
---------+---------+---------+---------+---------+-
    EMP_ID  EMP_LAST_NAME       EMP_FIRST_NAME
---------+---------+---------+---------+---------+-
      3333  FORD                JAMES
      9134  FRANKLIN            BRIANNA
      7777  HARRIS              ELISA
      3217  JOHNSON             EDWARD
DSNE610I NUMBER OF ROWS DISPLAYED IS 4
```

## SUBQUERY

A subquery is essentially a query within a query. Suppose for example we want to list the employee or employees who make the largest salary in the company. You can use a subquery to determine the maximum salary, and then use that value in the WHERE clause.

```
SELECT EMP_ID, EMP_REGULAR_PAY
FROM EMP_PAY
WHERE EMP_REGULAR_PAY
   = (SELECT MAX(EMP_REGULAR_PAY)
        FROM EMP_PAY);
---------+---------+---------+---------+----
    EMP_ID  EMP_REGULAR_PAY
---------+---------+---------+---------+----
      7459          85000.00
DSNE610I NUMBER OF ROWS DISPLAYED IS 1
```

What if there is more than one employee who makes the highest salary? Let's bump two people up to 85000 (and 4500 bonus) and see.

```
UPDATE EMP_PAY
SET EMP_REGULAR_PAY = 85000.00,
    EMP_BONUS_PAY = 4500
WHERE EMP_ID IN (4720,9134);
```

Here are the results:

```
    SELECT * FROM EMP_PAY;
---------+---------+---------+---------+----
    EMP_ID   EMP_REGULAR_PAY   EMP_BONUS_PAY
---------+---------+---------+---------+----
       3217           65000.00          5500.00
       7459           85000.00          4500.00
       9134           85000.00          4500.00
       4720           85000.00          4500.00
       6288           70000.00          2000.00
DSNE610I NUMBER OF ROWS DISPLAYED IS 5
```

Now let's see if our subquery still works:

```
    SELECT EMP_ID, EMP_REGULAR_PAY
    FROM EMP_PAY
    WHERE EMP_REGULAR_PAY
       = (SELECT MAX(EMP_REGULAR_PAY)
           FROM EMP_PAY);
---------+---------+---------+---------+----
    EMP_ID   EMP_REGULAR_PAY
---------+---------+---------+---------+----
       7459           85000.00
       9134           85000.00
       4720           85000.00
DSNE610I NUMBER OF ROWS DISPLAYED IS 3
```

The query pulls all three of the highest paid employees. Subqueries are very powerful in that any value you can produce via a subquery can be substituted into a main query as selection or exclusion criteria.

## GROUP BY

You can summarize data using the GROUP BY clause. For example, let's determine how many distinct employee salary rates there are and how many employees are paid those amounts.

```
    SELECT EMP_REGULAR_PAY,
      COUNT(*) AS "HOW MANY"
      FROM EMP_PAY
      GROUP BY EMP_REGULAR_PAY;

---------+---------+---------+---------+-
EMP_REGULAR_PAY    HOW MANY
---------+---------+---------+---------+-
       65000.00          1
       70000.00          1
       85000.00          3
DSNE610I NUMBER OF ROWS DISPLAYED IS 3
```

54

## ORDER BY

You can sort the display into ascending or descending sequence using the ORDER BY clause. To take the query we were just using for the group-by, let's present the data in descending sequence:

```
SELECT EMP_REGULAR_PAY,
COUNT(*) AS "HOW MANY"
FROM EMP_PAY
GROUP BY EMP_REGULAR_PAY
ORDER BY EMP_REGULAR_PAY DESC

---------+---------+---------+---------+-----
EMP_REGULAR_PAY     HOW MANY
---------+---------+---------+---------+-----
     85000.00          3
     70000.00          1
     65000.00          1
DSNE610I NUMBER OF ROWS DISPLAYED IS 3
```

## HAVING

You could also use the GROUP BY with a HAVING clause that limits the results to only those groups that meet another condition. Let's specify that the group must have more than one employee in it to be included in the results.

```
SELECT EMP_REGULAR_PAY,
COUNT(*) AS "HOW MANY"
FROM EMP_PAY
GROUP BY EMP_REGULAR_PAY
HAVING COUNT(*) > 1
ORDER BY EMP_REGULAR_PAY DESC;

---------+---------+---------+---------+-
EMP_REGULAR_PAY     HOW MANY
---------+---------+---------+---------+-
     85000.00          3
DSNE610I NUMBER OF ROWS DISPLAYED IS 1
```

Or if you want pay rates that have only one employee you could specify the count 1.

```
SELECT EMP_REGULAR_PAY,
   COUNT(*) AS "HOW MANY"
   FROM EMP_PAY
   GROUP BY EMP_REGULAR_PAY
   HAVING COUNT(*) = 1
   ORDER BY EMP_REGULAR_PAY DESC

---------+---------+---------+---------+------
```

```
EMP_REGULAR_PAY      HOW MANY
---------+---------+---------+---------+---------+------
       70000.00             1
       65000.00             1
DSNE610I NUMBER OF ROWS DISPLAYED IS 2
```

Before we move on, let's reset our two employees to whom we gave a temporary raise. Otherwise our EMP_PAY and EMP_PAY_CHECK tables will not be in sync.

```
UPDATE EMP_PAY
SET EMP_REGULAR_PAY = 80000.00, EMP_BONUS_PAY = 2500
WHERE EMP_ID = 4720;

UPDATE EMP_PAY
SET EMP_REGULAR_PAY = 75000.00, EMP_BONUS_PAY = 2500
WHERE EMP_ID = 9134;
```

Now our EMP_PAY table is restored:

```
  SELECT * FROM EMP_PAY;
---------+---------+---------+---------+--------
    EMP_ID  EMP_REGULAR_PAY  EMP_BONUS_PAY
---------+---------+---------+---------+--------
      3217         65000.00        5500.00
      7459         85000.00        4500.00
      9134         75000.00        2500.00
      4720         80000.00        2500.00
      6288         70000.00        2000.00
DSNE610I NUMBER OF ROWS DISPLAYED IS 5
```

## CASE Expressions

In some situations you may need to code more complex conditional logic into your queries. Assume we have a requirement to report all employees according to seniority. We've invented the classifications ENTRY, ADVANCED and SENIOR. We want to report those who have less than a year service as ENTRY, employees who have a year or more service but less than 5 years as ADVANCED, and all employees with 5 years or more service as SENIOR. Here is a sample query that performs this using a CASE expression:

```
  SELECT EMP_ID,
  EMP_LAST_NAME,
  EMP_FIRST_NAME,
  CASE
     WHEN EMP_SERVICE_YEARS  < 1 THEN 'ENTRY'
     WHEN EMP_SERVICE_YEARS  < 5 THEN 'ADVANCED'
     ELSE 'SENIOR'
  END CASE
  FROM HRSCHEMA.EMPLOYEE;
```

```
---------+---------+---------+---------+---------+---------+------
    EMP_ID   EMP_LAST_NAME          EMP_FIRST_NAME          CASE
---------+---------+---------+---------+---------+---------+------
      3217   JOHNSON                EDWARD                  SENIOR
      7459   STEWART                BETTY                   SENIOR
      9134   FRANKLIN               BRIANNA                 ENTRY
      4720   SCHULTZ                TIM                     SENIOR
      6288   WILLARD                JOE                     SENIOR
      3333   FORD                   JAMEs                   SENIOR
      7777   HARRIS                 ELISA                   ADVANCED
DSNE610I NUMBER OF ROWS DISPLAYED IS 7
```

You'll notice that the column heading for the case result is CASE. If you want to use a more meaningful column heading, then instead of closing the CASE statement with END CASE, close it with END AS <some literal>. So if we want to call the result of the CASE expression an employee's "LEVEL", code it this way:

```
SELECT EMP_ID,
EMP_LAST_NAME,
EMP_FIRST_NAME,
CASE
   WHEN EMP_SERVICE_YEARS  < 1 THEN 'ENTRY'
   WHEN EMP_SERVICE_YEARS  < 5 THEN 'ADVANCED'
   ELSE 'SENIOR'
END AS LEVEL
FROM HRSCHEMA.EMPLOYEE ;
```

```
---------+---------+---------+---------+---------+---------+-------
    EMP_ID   EMP_LAST_NAME          EMP_FIRST_NAME          LEVEL
---------+---------+---------+---------+---------+---------+-------
      3217   JOHNSON                EDWARD                  SENIOR
      7459   STEWART                BETTY                   SENIOR
      9134   FRANKLIN               BRIANNA                 ENTRY
      4720   SCHULTZ                TIM                     SENIOR
      6288   WILLARD                JOE                     SENIOR
      3333   FORD                   JAMEs                   SENIOR
      7777   HARRIS                 ELISA                   ADVANCED
DSNE610I NUMBER OF ROWS DISPLAYED IS 7
```

## JOINS

Now let's look at some cases where we need to pull data from more than one table. To do this we can use a join. Before we start running queries I want to add one row to the EMP_PAY_CHECK table. This is needed to make some of the joins work later, so bear with me.

```
INSERT INTO EMP_PAY_CHECK
VALUES
(7033,
77000.00,
77000 / 24);
```

Now our EMP_PAY_CHECK table has these rows.

```
   SELECT * FROM EMP_PAY_CHECK;
---------+---------+---------+---------+------
   EMP_ID   EMP_REGULAR_PAY   EMP_SEMIMTH_PAY
---------+---------+---------+---------+------
     3217          65000.00          2708.33
     7459          85000.00          3541.66
     9134          75000.00          3125.00
     4720          80000.00          3333.33
     6288          70000.00          2916.66
     7033          77000.00          3208.00
DSNE610I NUMBER OF ROWS DISPLAYED IS 6
```

## Inner joins

An inner join combines each row of one table with matching rows of the other table, keeping only the rows in which the join condition is true. You can join more than two tables but keep in mind that the more tables you join, the more record I/O is required and this could be a performance consideration. When I say a "performance consideration" I do not mean it is necessarily a problem. I mean it is one factor of many to keep in mind when designing an application process.

Let's do an example of a join. Assume we want a report that includes employee id, first and last names and pay rate for each employee. To accomplish this we need data from both the EMPLOYEE and the EMP_PAY tables. We can match the tables on EMP_ID which is the column they have in common.

We can perform our join either implicitly or with the JOIN verb (explicitly). In the first example will do the join implicitly by specifying we want to include rows for which the EMP_ID in the EMPLOYEE table matches the EMP_ID in the EMP_PAY table. The join is specified by the equality in the WHERE condition: WHERE A.EMP_ID = B.EMP_ID.

```
 SELECT A.EMP_ID,
 A.EMP_LAST_NAME,
 A.EMP_FIRST_NAME,
 B.EMP_REGULAR_PAY
 FROM HRSCHEMA.EMPLOYEE A, HRSCHEMA.EMP_PAY B
 WHERE A.EMP_ID = B.EMP_ID
 ORDER BY EMP_ID

 ---------+---------+---------+---------+---------+---------+---------+---
```

```
     EMP_ID   EMP_LAST_NAME        EMP_FIRST_NAME        EMP_REGULAR_PAY
---------+---------+---------+---------+---------+---------+---------+---
     3217   JOHNSON              EDWARD                      65000.00
     4720   SCHULTZ              TIM                         80000.00
     6288   WILLARD              JOE                         70000.00
     7459   STEWART              BETTY                       85000.00
     9134   FRANKLIN             BRIANNA                     75000.00
DSNE610I NUMBER OF ROWS DISPLAYED IS 5
```

Notice that in the SQL the column names are prefixed with a tag that is associated with the table being referenced. This is needed in all cases where the column being referenced exists in both tables (using the same column name). In this case, if you do not specify the qualifying tag, you will get an error that your column name reference is ambiguous, i.e., DB2 does not know which column from which table you are referencing.

Moving on, you can use an explicit join by specifying the JOIN or INNER JOIN verbs. This is actually a best practice because it helps keep the query clearer for those developers who follow you, especially as your queries get more complex.

```
SELECT A.EMP_ID,
A.EMP_LAST_NAME,
A.EMP_FIRST_NAME,
B.EMP_REGULAR_PAY
FROM HRSCHEMA.EMPLOYEE A
INNER JOIN
HRSCHEMA.EMP_PAY B
ON A.EMP_ID = B.EMP_ID
ORDER BY EMP_ID
---------+---------+---------+---------+---------+---------+---------+---
     EMP_ID   EMP_LAST_NAME        EMP_FIRST_NAME        EMP_REGULAR_PAY
---------+---------+---------+---------+---------+---------+---------+---
     3217   JOHNSON              EDWARD                      65000.00
     4720   SCHULTZ              TIM                         80000.00
     6288   WILLARD              JOE                         70000.00
     7459   STEWART              BETTY                       85000.00
     9134   FRANKLIN             BRIANNA                     75000.00
DSNE610I NUMBER OF ROWS DISPLAYED IS 5
```

Finally let's do a join with three tables just to extend the concepts. We'll join the EMPLOYEE, EMP_PAY and EMP_PAY_HIST tables for pay date February 15 as follows:

```
SELECT A.EMP_ID,
A.EMP_LAST_NAME,
B.EMP_REGULAR_PAY,
C.EMP_PAY_AMT
FROM HRSCHEMA.EMPLOYEE A
   INNER JOIN
     HRSCHEMA.EMP_PAY  B ON A.EMP_ID = B.EMP_ID
   INNER JOIN
     HRSCHEMA.EMP_PAY_HIST C ON B.EMP_ID = C.EMP_ID
WHERE C.EMP_PAY_DATE = '2/15/2017'
```

```
---------+---------+---------+---------+---------+---------+-----
    EMP_ID  EMP_LAST_NAME         EMP_REGULAR_PAY  EMP_PAY_AMT
---------+---------+---------+---------+---------+---------+-----
      3217  JOHNSON                     65000.00     2708.33
      7459  STEWART                     85000.00     3541.66
      9134  FRANKLIN                    75000.00     3125.00
      4720  SCHULTZ                     80000.00     3333.33
      6288  WILLARD                     70000.00     2916.66
DSNE610I NUMBER OF ROWS DISPLAYED IS 5
```

Now let's move on to outer joins. There are three types of outer joins. A **left outer join** includes matching rows from both tables plus any rows from the first table (the LEFT table) that were missing from the other table but that otherwise satisfied the WHERE condition. A **right outer join** includes matching rows from both tables plus any rows from the second (the RIGHT) table that were missing from the join but that otherwise satisfied the WHERE condition. A **full outer join** includes matching rows from both tables, plus those in either table that were not matched but which otherwise satisfied the WHERE condition. We'll look at examples of all three types of outer joins.

## Left Outer Join

Let's try a left outer join to include matching rows from the EMPLOYEE and EMP_PAY tables, plus any rows in the EMPLOYEE table that might not be in the EMP_PAY table. In this case we are not using a WHERE clause because the table is very small and we want to see all the results. But keep in mind that we could use a WHERE clause to add additional conditions.

```
SELECT A.EMP_ID,
A.EMP_LAST_NAME,
A.EMP_FIRST_NAME,
B.EMP_REGULAR_PAY
FROM HRSCHEMA.EMPLOYEE A
LEFT OUTER JOIN
HRSCHEMA.EMP_PAY B
ON A.EMP_ID = B.EMP_ID
ORDER BY EMP_ID;


---------+---------+---------+---------+---------+---------+---------+---
    EMP_ID  EMP_LAST_NAME       EMP_FIRST_NAME       EMP_REGULAR_PAY
---------+---------+---------+---------+---------+---------+---------+---
      3217  JOHNSON             EDWARD                      65000.00
      3333  FORD                JAMES                ---------------
      4720  SCHULTZ             TIM                         80000.00
      6288  WILLARD             JOE                         70000.00
      7459  STEWART             BETTY                       85000.00
      7777  HARRIS              ELISA                ---------------
      9134  FRANKLIN            BRIANNA                     75000.00
DSNE610I NUMBER OF ROWS DISPLAYED IS 7
```

As you can see, we've included two employees who have not been assigned an annual salary yet. James Ford and Elisa Harris have NULL as their regular pay. The LEFT JOIN says we

60

want all records in the first (left) table that satisfy the query even if there is no matching record in the right table. That's why the query results included the two unmatched records.

Let's do another left join, and this time we'll join the EMPLOYEE table with the EMP_PAY_CHECK table. Like before, we want all records from the EMPLOYEE and EMP_PAY_CHECK tables that match on EMP_ID, plus any EMPLOYEE records that could not be matched to EMP_PAY_CHECK.

```
SELECT A.EMP_ID,
A.EMP_LAST_NAME,
A.EMP_FIRST_NAME,
B.EMP_SEMIMTH_PAY
FROM HRSCHEMA.EMPLOYEE A
LEFT OUTER JOIN
HRSCHEMA.EMP_PAY_CHECK B
ON A.EMP_ID = B.EMP_ID
ORDER BY EMP_ID;
```

| EMP_ID | EMP_LAST_NAME | EMP_FIRST_NAME | EMP_SEMIMTH_PAY |
|---|---|---|---|
| 3217 | JOHNSON | EDWARD | 2708.33 |
| 3333 | FORD | JAMEs | --------------- |
| 4720 | SCHULTZ | TIM | 3333.33 |
| 6288 | WILLARD | JOE | 2916.66 |
| 7459 | STEWART | BETTY | 3541.66 |
| 7777 | HARRIS | ELISA | --------------- |
| 9134 | FRANKLIN | BRIANNA | 3125.00 |

DSNE610I NUMBER OF ROWS DISPLAYED IS 7

Again we find two records in the EMPLOYEE table with no matching EMP_PAY_CHECK records. From a business standpoint that could be a problem unless the two are new hires who have not received their first pay check.

## Right Outer Join

Meanwhile, now let us turn it around and do a right join. In this case we want all matching records in the EMPLOYEE and EMP_PAY_CHECK records plus any unmatched records in the EMP_PAY_CHECK table (the right hand table). We could also add a WHERE condition such that the EMP_SEMIMTH_PAY column has to be populated (cannot be NULL). Let's do that.

```
SELECT B.EMP_ID,
A.EMP_LAST_NAME,
A.EMP_FIRST_NAME,
B.EMP_SEMIMTH_PAY
FROM HRSCHEMA.EMPLOYEE A
   RIGHT OUTER JOIN
      HRSCHEMA.EMP_PAY_CHECK B
         ON A.EMP_ID = B.EMP_ID
WHERE EMP_SEMIMTH_PAY IS NOT NULL;
```

```
---------+---------+---------+---------+---------+---------+---------+---
   EMP_ID   EMP_LAST_NAME        EMP_FIRST_NAME        EMP_SEMIMTH_PAY
---------+---------+---------+---------+---------+---------+---------+---
     3217   JOHNSON              EDWARD                       2708.33
     4720   SCHULTZ              TIM                          3333.33
     6288   WILLARD              JOE                          2916.66
     7033   --------------------  --------------------        3208.00
     7459   STEWART              BETTY                        3541.66
     9134   FRANKLIN             BRIANNA                      3125.00
DSNE610I NUMBER OF ROWS DISPLAYED IS 6
```

Now we have a case where there is a record in the EMP_PAY_CHECK table for employee 7033, but that same employee number is NOT in the EMPLOYEE table. That is absolutely something to research! It is important to find out why this condition exists (of course we know it exists because we intentionally added an unmatched record to set up the example).

Outer joins are a very useful tool in tracking down data discrepancies between tables (subqueries are another useful tool). Keep this example in mind when you are called on by your boss or your client to troubleshoot a data integrity problem in a high pressure, time sensitive situation. You need all the tools you can get.

**Full Outer Join**

Finally, let's do a full outer join to include both matched and unmatched records from both tables that meet the where condition. This will expose all the discrepancies we already uncovered, but now we'll do it with a single query.

```
     SELECT A.EMP_ID,
       A.EMP_LAST_NAME,
       B.EMP_SEMIMTH_PAY
       FROM EMPLOYEE A
          FULL OUTER JOIN
             EMP_PAY_CHECK B
                ON A.EMP_ID = B.EMP_ID;
---------+---------+---------+---------+---------+--
   EMP_ID   EMP_LAST_NAME        EMP_SEMIMTH_PAY
---------+---------+---------+---------+---------+--
     3217   JOHNSON                      2708.33
     3333   FORD                 ---------------
     4720   SCHULTZ                      3333.33
     6288   WILLARD                      2916.66
-----------  --------------------        3208.00
     7459   STEWART                      3541.66
     7777   HARRIS               ---------------
     9134   FRANKLIN                     3125.00
DSNE610I NUMBER OF ROWS DISPLAYED IS 8
```

So with the FULL OUTER join we have identified the missing EMPLOYEE record, as well as the two EMP_PAY_CHECK records that may be missing. Again these examples are intended both to explain the difference between the join types, and also to lend support to troubleshooting efforts where data integrity is involved.

## UNION and INTERSECT

Another way to combine the results from two or more tables (or in some complex cases, to combine different result sets from a single table) is to use the UNION and INTERSECT statements. In some cases this can be preferable to doing a join.

### Union

The UNION predicate combines the result sets from sub-SELECT queries. To understand how this might be useful, let's look at three examples. First, let's say we have two companies that have merged to form a third company. We have two tables EMP_COMPA and EMP_COMPB that we have structured with an EMP_ID, EMP_LAST_NAME and EMP_FIRST_NAME. We are going to structure a third table which will create all new employee ids by generation using an identity column. The DDL for the new table looks like this:

```
CREATE TABLE HRSCHEMA.EMPLOYEE_NEW(
EMP_ID INT GENERATED ALWAYS AS IDENTITY,
EMP_OLD_ID INTEGER,
EMP_LAST_NAME VARCHAR(30) NOT NULL,
EMP_FIRST_NAME VARCHAR(20) NOT NULL)
IN TSHR;
```

Now we can load the table using a UNION as follows:

```
INSERT INTO
HRSCHEMA.EMPLOYEE_NEW

SELECT EMP_ID,
EMP_LAST_NAME,
EMP_FIRST_NAME
FROM HRSCHEMA.EMP_COMPA

UNION

SELECT EMP_ID,
EMP_LAST_NAME,
EMP_FIRST_NAME
FROM HRSCHEMA.EMP_COMPB;
```

This will load the new table with data from both the old tables, and the new employee numbers will be auto-generated. Notice that by design we keep the old employee numbers for cross reference if needed.

When using a UNION, the column list must be identical in terms of the number of columns and data types, but the column names need not be the same. The UNION operation looks at the columns by position in the subqueries, not by name.

Let's look at two other examples of UNION queries. First, recall that earlier we used a full outer join to return all employee ids, including those that exist in one table but not the other.

```
SELECT A.EMP_ID,
B.EMP_ID,
A.EMP_LAST_NAME,
B.EMP_SEMIMTH_PAY
FROM HRSCHEMA.EMPLOYEE A
    FULL OUTER JOIN
        HRSCHEMA.EMP_PAY_CHECK B
            ON A.EMP_ID = B.EMP_ID;
```

If we just needed a unique list of employee id numbers from the EMPLOYEE and EMP_PAY_CHECK tables, we could instead use this UNION SQL:

```
SELECT EMP_ID
FROM HRSCHEMA.EMPLOYEE
UNION
SELECT EMP_ID
FROM HRSCHEMA.EMP_PAY_CHECK
```

```
---------+---------+---------+---------+-
    EMP_ID
---------+---------+---------+---------+-
      3217
      3333
      4720
      6288
      7033
      7459
      7777
      9134
DSNE610I NUMBER OF ROWS DISPLAYED IS 8
```

If you are wondering why we didn't get duplicate employee numbers in our list, it is because the UNION statement automatically eliminates duplicates. If for some reason you need to retain the duplicates, you would need to specify UNION ALL.

One final example will show how handy the UNION predicate is. Suppose that you want to query the EMPLOYEE table to get a list of all employee names for an upcoming company party. But you also have a contractor who (by business rules) cannot be in the EMPLOYEE table. You still want to include the contractor's name in the result set for whom to invite to the party. Let's say you want to identify the contractor with a pseudo-employee-id of 9999, and the contractor's name is Janet Ko.

You could code the query as follows:

```
SELECT EMP_ID,
EMP_LAST_NAME,
EMP_FIRST_NAME
FROM HRSCHEMA.EMPLOYEE
UNION
SELECT 9999,
'KO',
'JANET'
FROM SYSIBM.SYSDUMMY1;
```

```
---------+---------+---------+---------+-----
    EMP_ID  EMP_LAST_NAME EMP_FIRST_NAME
---------+---------+---------+---------+-----
      3217  JOHNSON          EDWARD
      3333  FORD             JAMES
      4720  SCHULTZ          TIM
      6288  WILLARD          JOE
      7459  STEWART          BETTY
      7777  HARRIS           ELISA
      9134  FRANKLIN         BRIANNA
      9999  KO               JANET
DSNE610I NUMBER OF ROWS DISPLAYED IS 8
```

Now you have listed all the employees plus your contractor friend Janet on your query results. This is a useful technique when you have a "mostly" table driven system that also has some exceptions to the business rules. Sometimes a system has one-off situations that simply don't justify full blown changes to the system design. UNION can help in these cases.

### Intersect

The INTERSECT predicate returns a combined result set that consists of all of the matching rows (existing in **both** result sets). In one of the earlier UNION examples, we wanted all employee ids as long as they existed in either the EMPLOYEE table or the EMP_PAY_CHECK table.

```
SELECT EMP_ID
FROM HRSCHEMA.EMPLOYEE
UNION
SELECT EMP_ID
FROM HRSCHEMA.EMP_PAY_CHECK
```

```
---------+---------+---------
     EMP_ID
---------+---------+---------
      3217
      4720
      6288
      7033
      7459
      9134
```

Now let's say we only want a list of employee ids that appear in both tables. The INTERSECT will accomplish that for us and we only need to change that one word in the query:

```
SELECT EMP_ID
FROM HRSCHEMA.EMPLOYEE
INTERSECT
SELECT EMP_ID
FROM HRSCHEMA.EMP_PAY_CHECK;
```

```
---------+---------+---------+---------+--------
     EMP_ID
---------+---------+---------+---------+--------
      3217
      4720
      6288
      7459
      9134
DSNE610I NUMBER OF ROWS DISPLAYED IS 5
```

### Common Table Expression

A common table expression is a result set that you can create and then reference in a query as though it were a table. It sometimes makes coding easier. Here's an example. Suppose we need to work with an aggregated year-to-date total pay for each employee. Recall that our table named EMPL_PAY_HIST includes these fields:

```
(EMP_ID INTEGER NOT NULL,
EMP_PAY_DATE DATE NOT NULL,
EMP_PAY_AMT DECIMAL (8,2) NOT NULL);
```

Assume further that we have created the following SQL that includes aggregated totals for the employees' pay:

```
WITH EMP_PAY_SUM (EMP_ID, EMP_PAY_TOTAL) AS
(SELECT EMP_ID,
SUM(EMP_PAY_AMT)
AS EMP_PAY_TOTAL
FROM EMP_PAY_HIST
GROUP BY EMP_ID)

SELECT B.EMP_ID,
A.EMP_LAST_NAME,
A.EMP_FIRST_NAME,
B.EMP_PAY_TOTAL
FROM EMPLOYEE A
INNER JOIN
EMP_PAY_SUM B
ON A.EMP_ID = B.EMP_ID;
```

What we've done is to create a temporary result set named EMP_PAY_SUM that can be queried by SQL as if it were a table. This helps break down the data requirement into two pieces, one of which summarizes the pay data and the other of which joins columns from other tables.

Here's the result of our common table expression and the query against it.

```
WITH EMP_PAY_SUM (EMP_ID, EMP_PAY_TOTAL) AS
(SELECT EMP_ID,
SUM(EMP_PAY_AMT)
AS EMP_PAY_TOTAL
FROM EMP_PAY_HIST
GROUP BY EMP_ID)

SELECT B.EMP_ID,
A.EMP_LAST_NAME,
A.EMP_FIRST_NAME,
B.EMP_PAY_TOTAL
FROM EMPLOYEE A
INNER JOIN
EMP_PAY_SUM B
ON A.EMP_ID = B.EMP_ID;


---------+---------+---------+---------+---------+---------+---------+-------
    EMP_ID  EMP_LAST_NAME  EMP_FIRST_NAME              EMP_PAY_TOTAL
---------+---------+---------+---------+---------+---------+---------+-------
      3217  JOHNSON        EDWARD                           10833.32
      4720  SCHULTZ        TIM                              13333.32
      6288  WILLARD        JOE                              11666.64
      7459  STEWART        BETTY                            14166.64
      9134  FRANKLIN       BRIANNA                          12500.00
DSNE610I NUMBER OF ROWS DISPLAYED IS 5
```

This example may not seem like much because you could have easily combined the two SQLs into one. But as your data stores get more numerous, and your queries and joins grow more complex, you may find that common table expressions can simplify queries both for you and for the developer that follows you.

# XML

XML is a highly used standard for exchanging self-describing data files or documents. Even if you work in a shop that does not use the DB2 XML data type or XML functions, it is good to know how to use these. A complete tutorial on XML is well beyond the scope of this book. We'll review some XML basics, but if you have little or no experience with XML, I strongly suggest that you purchase some books to acquire this knowledge. The following are a few that can help fill in the basics:

XML in a Nutshell, Third Edition 3rd Edition by Elliotte Rusty Harold (ISBN 978-0596007645)

XSLT 2.0 and XPath 2.0 Programmer's Reference by Michael Kay (ISBN: 978-0470192740)

XQuery: Search Across a Variety of XML Data by Priscilla Walmsley
(ISBN: ISBN-13: 978-1491915103)

## Basic XML Concepts

You may know that XML stands for Extensible Markup Language. XML technology is cross-platform and independent of machine and software. It provides a structure that consists of both data and data element tags, and so it describes the data in both human readable and machine readable format. The tag names for the elements are defined by the developer/user of the data.

## XML Structure

XML has a tree type structure that is required to begin with a root element and then it expands to the branches. To continue our discussion of the EMPLOYEE domain, let's take a simple XML example with an employee profile as the root. We'll include the employee id, the address and birth date. The XML document might look like this:

```
<?xml version="1.0" encoding="UTF-8"?>
<EMP_PROFILE>
      <EMP_ID>4175</EMP_ID>
      <EMP_ADDRESS>
            <STREET>6161 MARGARET LANE</STREET>
            <CITY>ERINDALE</CITY>
            <STATE>AR</STATE>
            <ZIP_CODE>72653</ZIP_CODE>
      </EMP_ADDRESS>
      <BIRTH_DATE>07/14/1991</BIRTH_DATE>
</EMP_PROFILE>
```

XML documents frequently begin with a declaration which includes the XML version and the encoding scheme of the document. In our example, we are using XML version 1.0 which is still very common. This declaration is optional but it's a best practice to include it.

Notice after the version specification that we continue with the tag name EMP_PROFILE enclosed by the <> symbols. The employee profile element ends with /EMP_PROFILE enclosed by the <> symbols. Similarly each sub-element is tagged and enclosed and the value (if any) appears between the opening and closing of the element.

XML documents must have a single root element, i.e., one element that is the root of all other elements. If you want more than one EMP_PROFILE in a document, then you would need a higher level element to contain the profiles. For example you could have a DEPARTMENT element that contains employee profiles, and a COMPANY element that contains DEPARTMENTS.

All elements must have a closing tag. Elements that are not populated can be represented by an opening and closing with nothing in between. For example, if an employee's birthday is not known, it can be represented by <BIRTH_DATE></BIRTH_DATE> or you can use the short hand form <BIRTH_DATE/>.

The example document includes elements such as the employee id, address and birth date. The address is broken down into a street name, city, state and zip code. Comments can be included in an XML document by following the following format:

```
<!-- This is a sample comment -->
```

By default, white space is preserved in XML documents.

Ok, so we've given you a drive-thru version of XML. We have almost enough information to move on to how to manipulate XML data in DB2. Before we get to that, let's briefly look at two XML-related technologies that we will need.

## XML Related Technologies

### XPath
The extensible path language (XPath) is used to locate and extract information from an XML document using "path" expressions through the XML nodes. For example, in the case of the employee XML document we created earlier, you could locate and return a zip code value by specifying the path.

Recall this structure:

```
<EMP_PROFILE>
    <EMP_ID>4175</EMP_ID>
    <EMP_ADDRESS>
        <STREET>6161 MARGARET LANE</STREET>
        <CITY>ERINDALE</CITY>
```

```
        <STATE>AR</STATE>
        <ZIP_CODE>72653</ZIP_CODE>
    </EMP_ADDRESS>
    <BIRTH_DATE>07/14/1991</BIRTH_DATE>
</EMP_PROFILE>
```

In this example, the employee profile nodes with zip code 72653 can be identified using the following path:

```
/EMP_PROFILE/ADDRESS[ZIP_CODE=72653]
```

The XPath expression for all employees who live in Texas as follows:

```
/EMP_PROFILE/ADDRESS[STATE="TX"]
```

## XQuery

XQuery enables us to query XML data using XPath expressions. It is similar to how we query relational data using SQL, but of course the syntax is different. Here's an example of pulling the employee id of every employee who lives at a zip code greater than 90000 from an XML document named **employees.xml**.

```
for $x in doc("employees.xml")employee/profile/address/zipcode
where $x/zipcode>90000
order by $x/zipcode
return $x/empid
```

In DB2 you run an XQuery using the built-in function **XMLQUERY**. We'll show you some examples using XMLQUERY shortly.

## DB2 Support for XML

The pureXML technology provides support for XML under DB2 for z/OS. DB2 includes an XML data type and many built-in DB2 functions to validate, traverse and manipulate XML data. The DB2 XML data type can store well-formed XML documents in their hierarchical form and retrieve entire documents or portions of documents.

You can execute DML operations such as inserting, updating and deleting XML documents. You can index and create triggers on XML columns. Finally, you can extract data items from an XML document and then store those values in columns of relational tables using the SQL XMLTABLE built-in function.

# XML Examples

## XML for the EMPLOYEE table

Suppose that we need to implement a new interface with our employee benefits providers who use XML as the data exchange format. This could give us a reason to store our detailed employee information in an XML structure within the EMPLOYEE table. For our purposes, we will add a column named EMP_PROFILE to the EMPLOYEE table and make it an XML column. Here's the DDL:

```
ALTER TABLE HRSCHEMA.EMPLOYEE
ADD COLUMN EMP_PROFILE XML;
```

We could also establish an XML schema to validate our data structure, but for the moment we'll just deal with the basic SQL operations. As long as the XML is well formed, DB2 will accept it without a schema to validate against.

Let's assume we are going to add a record to the EMPLOYEE table for employee Fred Turnbull who has employee id 4175, has 1 year if service and was promoted on 12/1/2016. Here's a sample XML document structure we want for storing the employee profile:

```
<EMP_PROFILE>
<EMP_ID>4175</EMP_ID>
<EMP_ADDRESS>
<STREET>6161 MARGARET LANE</STREET>
<CITY>ERINDALE</CITY>
<STATE>AR</STATE>
<ZIP_CODE>72653</ZIP_CODE>
</EMP_ADDRESS>
<BIRTH_DATE>07/14/1991</BIRTH_DATE>
</EMP_PROFILE>
```

## INSERT With XML

Now we can insert the new record as follows:

```
INSERT INTO HRSCHEMA.EMPLOYEE
(EMP_ID,
 EMP_LAST_NAME,
 EMP_FIRST_NAME,
 EMP_SERVICE_YEARS,
 EMP_PROMOTION_DATE,
 EMP_PROFILE)
VALUES (4175,
'TURNBULL',
'FRED',
1,
'12/01/2016',
```

```
'
<EMP_PROFILE>
<EMP_ID>4175</EMP_ID>
<EMP_ADDRESS>
<STREET>6161 MARGARET LANE</STREET>
<CITY>ERINDALE</CITY>
<STATE>AR</STATE>
<ZIP_CODE>72653</ZIP_CODE>
</EMP_ADDRESS>
<BIRTH_DATE>07/14/1991</BIRTH_DATE>
</EMP_PROFILE>
');
```

## SELECT With XML

You can do a SELECT on an XML column and depending on what query tool you are using, you can display the content of the record in fairly readable form. Since the XML data is stored as one long string, it may be difficult to read in its entirety without reformatting. We'll look at some options for that later. Let's select the column we just added using SPUFI.

```
SELECT EMP_ID, EMP_PROFILE FROM HRSCHEMA.EMPLOYEE
WHERE EMP_ID = 4175;
-------+---------+---------+---------+---------+---------+---------+-----
   EMP_ID  EMP_PROFILE
-------+---------+---------+---------+---------+---------+---------+-----
    4175  <?xml version="1.0" encoding="IBM037"?><EMP_PROFILE><EMP_ID>41
```

In SPUFI, you would need to scroll to the right to see the rest of the column contents.

## UPDATE With XML

To update an XML column you can use standard SQL if you want to update the entire content of the column. Suppose we want to change the address. This SQL will do it:

```
UPDATE HRSCHEMA.EMPLOYEE
SET EMP_PROFILE
 = '<EMP_PROFILE>
          <EMP_ID>3217</EMP_ID>
          <EMP_ADDRESS>
          <STREET>2913 PATE DR</STREET>
          <CITY>FORT WORTH</CITY>
          <STATE>TX</STATE>
          <ZIP_CODE>76105</ZIP_CODE>
      </EMP_ADDRESS>
      <BIRTH_DATE>03/15/1952</BIRTH_DATE>
    </EMP_PROFILE>
    '
WHERE EMP_ID = 3217;
```

## DELETE With XML

If you wish to delete the entire EMP_PROFILE, you can set it to NULL as follows:

```
UPDATE HRSCHEMA.EMPLOYEE
SET EMP_PROFILE = NULL
WHERE EMP_ID = 3217;


SELECT EMP_ID, EMP_PROFILE FROM HRSCHEMA.EMPLOYEE
WHERE EMP_ID = 3217;
-------+---------+---------+---------+---------+---------+---------+-----
   EMP_ID  EMP_PROFILE
-------+---------+---------+---------+---------+---------+---------+-----
     3217  ------------------------------------------------------------
```

As you can see, the EMP_PROFILE column has been set to NULL. At this point, only one row in the EMPLOYEE table has the EMP_PROFILE populated.

```
SELECT EMP_ID, EMP_PROFILE FROM HRSCHEMA.EMPLOYEE;

-------+---------+---------+---------+---------+---------+---------+--------
   EMP_ID  EMP_PROFILE
-------+---------+---------+---------+---------+---------+---------+--------
     3217  ------------------------------------------------------------
     7459  ------------------------------------------------------------
     9134  ------------------------------------------------------------
     4175  <?xml version="1.0" encoding="IBM037"?><EMP_PROFILE><EMP_ID>4175<
```

Let's go ahead and add the XML data back to this record so we can use it later for other XML queries.

```
UPDATE HRSCHEMA.EMPLOYEE
SET EMP_PROFILE
 = '<EMP_PROFILE>
            <EMP_ID>3217</EMP_ID>
            <EMP_ADDRESS>
            <STREET>2913 PATE DR</STREET>
            <CITY>FORT WORTH</CITY>
            <STATE>TX</STATE>
            <ZIP_CODE>76105</ZIP_CODE>
      </EMP_ADDRESS>
      <BIRTH_DATE>03/15/1952</BIRTH_DATE>
    </EMP_PROFILE>
    '
WHERE EMP_ID = 3217;
```

Also, let's update one more record so we have a bit more data to work with.

```
UPDATE EMPLOYEE
SET EMP_PROFILE
```

```
 = '<EMP_PROFILE>
  <EMP_ID>7459</EMP_ID>
  <EMP_ADDRESS>
       <STREET>6742 OAK ST</STREET>
       <CITY>DALLAS</CITY>
       <STATE>TX</STATE>
       <ZIP_CODE>75277</ZIP_CODE>
  </EMP_ADDRESS>
  <BIRTH_DATE>09/22/1963</BIRTH_DATE>
/EMP_PROFILE> '
WHERE EMP_ID = 7459;
```

## XML BUILTIN FUNCTIONS

### XMLQUERY

XMLQUERY is the DB2 built-in function that enables you to run XQuery. Here is an example of using XMLQUERY with the XQuery **xmlcolumn** function to retrieve an XML element from the EMP_PROFILE element. In this case we will select the zip code for employee 4175.

```
SELECT XMLQUERY
('for $info
in db2-fn:xmlcolumn("HRSCHEMA.EMPLOYEE.EMP_PROFILE")/EMP_PROFILE
return $info/EMP_ADDRESS/ZIP_CODE') AS ZIPCODE
from HRSCHEMA.EMPLOYEE
where EMP_ID = 4175;


ZIPCODE
-------------------------
<ZIP_CODE>72653</ZIP_CODE>
```

Notice that the data is returned in XML format. If you don't want the data returned with its XML structure, simply add the XQuery text() function at the end of the return string, as below:

```
SELECT XMLQUERY
('for $info
in db2-fn:xmlcolumn("HRSCHEMA.EMPLOYEE.EMP_PROFILE")/EMP_PROFILE
return $info/EMP_ADDRESS/ZIP_CODE/text()') AS ZIPCODE
FROM HRSCHEMA.EMPLOYEE
WHERE EMP_ID = 4175;
```

The result of this query will not include the XML format.

```
ZIPCODE
-------
 72653
```

## XMLEXISTS

The XMLEXISTS predicate specifies an XQuery expression. If the XQuery expression returns an empty sequence, the value of the XMLEXISTS predicate is false. Otherwise, XMLEXISTS returns true and those rows matching the XMLEXISTS value of true are returned.

XMLEXISTS enables us to specify rows based on the XML content which is often what you want to do. Suppose you want to return the first and last names of all employees who live in the state of Texas? This query with XMLEXISTS would accomplish it:

```
SELECT EMP_LAST_NAME, EMP_FIRST_NAME
FROM HRSCHEMA.EMPLOYEE
WHERE
XMLEXISTS('$info/EMP_PROFILE[EMP_ADDRESS/STATE/text()="TX"]'
PASSING EMP_PROFILE AS "info");


---------+---------+---------+---------+---------+---------+---
EMP_LAST_NAME                      EMP_FIRST_NAME
---------+---------+---------+---------+---------+---------+---
JOHNSON                            EDWARD
STEWART                            BETTY
```

You can also use XMLEXISTS with update and delete functions.

## XMLSERIALIZE

The XMLSERIALIZE function returns a serialized XML value of the specified data type that is generated from the first argument. You can use this function to generate an XML structure from relational data. Here's an example.

```
SELECT E.EMP_ID,
XMLSERIALIZE(XMLELEMENT ( NAME "EMP_FULL_NAME",
   E.EMP_FIRST_NAME || ' ' || E.EMP_LAST_NAME)
             AS CLOB(100)) AS "RESULT"
    FROM HRSCHEMA.EMPLOYEE E;
---------+---------+---------+---------+---------+---------+-
    EMP_ID  RESULT
---------+---------+---------+---------+---------+---------+-
     3217  <EMP_FULL_NAME>EDWARD JOHNSON</EMP_FULL_NAME>
     7459  <EMP_FULL_NAME>BETTY STEWART</EMP_FULL_NAME>
     9134  <EMP_FULL_NAME>BRIANNA FRANKLIN</EMP_FULL_NAME>
     4175  <EMP_FULL_NAME>FRED TURNBULL</EMP_FULL_NAME>
     4720  <EMP_FULL_NAME>TIM SCHULTZ</EMP_FULL_NAME>
     6288  <EMP_FULL_NAME>JOE WILLARD</EMP_FULL_NAME>
     3333  <EMP_FULL_NAME>JAMEs FORD</EMP_FULL_NAME>
     7777  <EMP_FULL_NAME>ELISA HARRIS</EMP_FULL_NAME>
DSNE610I NUMBER OF ROWS DISPLAYED IS 8
```

## XMLTABLE

This function can be used to convert XML data to relational data. You can then use it for traditional SQL such as in joins. To use XMLTABLE you must specify the relational column names you want to use. Then you point these column names to the XML content using path expressions. For this example we'll pull address information from the profile:

```
SELECT X.*
FROM HRSCHEMA.EMPLOYEE,
XMLTABLE ('$x/EMP_PROFILE'
          PASSING EMP_PROFILE as "x"
  COLUMNS
    STREET   VARCHAR(20) PATH 'EMP_ADDRESS/STREET',
    CITY     VARCHAR(20) PATH 'EMP_ADDRESS/CITY',
    STATE    VARCHAR(02) PATH 'EMP_ADDRESS/STATE',
    ZIP      VARCHAR(10) PATH 'EMP_ADDRESS/ZIP_CODE')
    AS X
      ;
---------+---------+---------+---------+---------+---------+-
STREET                   CITY                 STATE  ZIP
---------+---------+---------+---------+---------+---------+-
2913 PATE DR             FORT WORTH            TX     76105
6742 OAK ST              DALLAS                TX     75277
6161 MARGARET LANE       ERINDALE              AR     72653
DSNE610I NUMBER OF ROWS DISPLAYED IS 3
```

## XMLMODIFY

XMLMODIFY allows you to make changes within the XML document. There are three expressions available for XMLMODIFY: insert, delete and replace. Here is a sample of using the replace expression to change the ZIP_CODE element of the EMP_ADDRESS for employee 4175:

```
UPDATE HRSCHEMA.EMPLOYEE
SET EMP_PROFILE
= XMLMODIFY('replace value of node
HRSCHEMA.EMPLOYEE/EMP_PROFILE/EMP_ADDRESS/ZIP_CODE
with "72652" ')
WHERE EMP_ID = 4175;
```

Now let's verify that the statement worked successfully by finding the zip code on EMP_ID 4175.

```
SELECT XMLQUERY
('for $info
in db2-fn:xmlcolumn("HRSCHEMA.EMPLOYEE.EMP_PROFILE")/EMP_PROFILE
return $info/EMP_ADDRESS/ZIP_CODE/text()') AS ZIPCODE
from HRSCHEMA.EMPLOYEE
where EMP_ID = 4175;
```

```
-----------------------------------------------
ZIPCODE
-----------------------------------------------
 72652
```

**Important:**  to use XMLMODIFY, you must have created the table in a universal table space (UTS). Otherwise you will receive this SQLCODE error when you try to use the XMLMODIFY function:

```
DSNT408I SQLCODE = -4730, ERROR:  INVALID SPECIFICATION OF XML COLUMN
EMPLOYEE.EMP_PROFILE IS NOT DEFINED IN THE XML VERSIONING
FORMAT,REASON 1
```

# SPECIAL REGISTERS

Special registers allow you to access detailed information about the DB2 instance settings as well as certain session information. CURRENT DATE is an example of a special register that is often used in programming (see example below). The following are SQL examples of some commonly used special registers. I suggest that you focus on these.

## CURRENT CLIENT_USERID

CURRENT CLIENT_USERID contains the value of the client user ID from the client information that is specified for the connection. In the following example, the TSO logon id of the user is HRSCHEMA.

```
SELECT CURRENT CLIENT_USERID
FROM SYSIBM.SYSDUMMY1;
---------+---------+---------

---------+---------+---------
HRSCHEMA
```

## CURRENT DATE

CURRENT DATE specifies a date that is based on a reading of the time-of-day clock when the SQL statement is executed at the current server. This is often used in application programs to establish the processing date.

```
SELECT CURRENT DATE
FROM SYSIBM.SYSDUMMY1;
---------+---------+--

---------+---------+--
2017-01-13
```

## CURRENT DEGREE

CURRENT DEGREE specifies the degree of parallelism for the execution of queries that are dynamically prepared by the application process. A value of "ANY" enables parallel processing. A value of 1 prohibits parallel processing. You can query for the value of the CURRENT DEGREE as follows:

```
SELECT CURRENT DEGREE
FROM SYSIBM.SYSDUMMY1;
---------+---------+-----

---------+---------+-----
1
```

## CURRENT MEMBER

CURRENT MEMBER specifies the member name of a current DB2 data sharing member on which a statement is executing. The value of CURRENT MEMBER is a character string. More information on data sharing is provided later.

## CURRENT OPTIMIZATION HINT

CURRENT OPTIMIZATION HINT specifies the user-defined optimization hint that DB2 should use to generate the access path for dynamic statements.

## CURRENT RULES

CURRENT RULES specifies whether certain SQL statements are executed in accordance with DB2 rules or the rules of the SQL standard.

```
SELECT CURRENT RULES
FROM SYSIBM.SYSDUMMY1;
---------+---------+----

---------+---------+----
DB2
```

## CURRENT SCHEMA

CURRENT SCHEMA specifies the schema name used to qualify unqualified database object references in dynamically prepared SQL statements.

```
SELECT CURRENT SCHEMA
FROM SYSIBM.SYSDUMMY1;
---------+---------+---

---------+---------+---
HRSCHEMA
```

## CURRENT SERVER

CURRENT SERVER specifies the location name of the current server.

```
SELECT CURRENT SERVER
FROM SYSIBM.SYSDUMMY1;
---------+---------+--------

---------+---------+--------
LOCRGNA
```

## CURRENT SQLID

CURRENT SQLID specifies the SQL authorization ID of the process.

```
SELECT CURRENT SQLID
FROM SYSIBM.SYSDUMMY1;
---------+---------+----

HRSCHEMA
```

## CURRENT TEMPORAL BUSINESS_TIME

The CURRENT TEMPORAL BUSINESS_TIME special register specifies a TIMESTAMP(12) value that is used in the default BUSINESS_TIME period specification for references to application-period temporal tables.

## CURRENT TEMPORAL SYSTEM_TIME

The CURRENT TEMPORAL SYSTEM_TIME special register specifies a TIMESTAMP(12) value that is used in the default SYSTEM_TIME period specification for references to system-period temporal tables.

## CURRENT TIME

The CURRENT TIME special register specifies a time that is based on a reading of the time-of-day clock when the SQL statement is executed at the current server.

```
SELECT CURRENT TIME
FROM SYSIBM.SYSDUMMY1;
---------+---------+----

10.12.12
```

## CURRENT TIMESTAMP

The CURRENT TIMESTAMP special register specifies a timestamp based on the time-of-day clock at the current server.

```
SELECT CURRENT TIMESTAMP
FROM SYSIBM.SYSDUMMY1;
---------+---------+--------

---------+---------+--------
2017-01-13-10.12.51.778225
```

## SESSION_USER

SESSION_USER specifies the primary authorization ID of the process.

```
SELECT SESSION_USER
FROM SYSIBM.SYSDUMMY1;
---------+---------+-----

HRSCHEMA
```

# Complete List of Special Registers

The DB2 special registers are listed below and are from the DB2 product documentation:

https://www.ibm.com/support/knowledgecenter/SSEPEK_11.0.0/sqlref/src/tpc/db2z_specialregistersintro.html

## CURRENT APPLICATION COMPATIBILITY
Specifies the application compatibility level support for dynamic SQL statements in the package.

## CURRENT APPLICATION ENCODING SCHEME
Specifies which encoding scheme is to be used for dynamic statements.

## CURRENT CLIENT_ACCTNG
Contains the value of the accounting string from the client information that is specified for the connection.

## CURRENT CLIENT_APPLNAME
Contains the value of the application name from the client information that is specified for the connection.

## CURRENT CLIENT_CORR_TOKEN
Contains the value of the client correlation token from the client information that is specified for the connection.

## CURRENT CLIENT_USERID
Contains the value of the client user ID from the client information that is specified for the connection.

## CURRENT CLIENT_WRKSTNNAME
Contains the value of the workstation name from the client information that is specified for the connection.

## CURRENT DATE
Specifies a date that is based on a reading of the time-of-day clock when the SQL statement is executed at the current server.

## CURRENT DEBUG MODE
Specifies the default value for the DEBUG MODE option when certain routines are created. The DEBUG MODE option specifies whether the routine should be built with the ability to run in debugging mode.

## CURRENT DECFLOAT ROUNDING MODE
Specifies the default rounding mode that is used for DECFLOAT values.

## CURRENT DEGREE
Specifies the degree of parallelism for the execution of queries that are dynamically prepared by the application process.

## CURRENT EXPLAIN MODE
Contains the values that control the EXPLAIN behavior in regards to eligible dynamic SQL statements.

## CURRENT GET_ACCEL_ARCHIVE
Special register specifies whether a dynamic SQL query that references a table that is archived on an accelerator server uses the archived data. The special register does not apply to static SQL queries.

## CURRENT LOCALE LC_CTYPE
Specifies the LC_CTYPE locale that will be used to execute SQL statements that use a built-in function that references a locale. Functions LCASE, UCASE, and TRANSLATE (with a single argument) refer to the locale when they are executed.

## CURRENT MAINTAINED TABLE TYPES FOR OPTIMIZATION
Specifies a value that identifies the types of objects that can be considered to optimize the processing of dynamic SQL queries. This register contains a keyword representing table types.

## CURRENT MEMBER
Specifies the member name of a current DB2 data sharing member on which a statement is executing. The value of CURRENT MEMBER is a character string.

## CURRENT OPTIMIZATION HINT
Specifies the user-defined optimization hint that DB2 should use to generate the access path for dynamic statements.

## CURRENT PACKAGE PATH
Specifies a value that identifies the path used to resolve references to packages that are used to execute SQL statements. This special register applies to both static and dynamic statements.

## CURRENT PACKAGESET
Specifies an empty string, a string of blanks, or the collection ID of the package that will be used to execute SQL statements.

## CURRENT PATH
Specifies the SQL path used to resolve unqualified data type names and function names in dynamically prepared SQL statements. It is also used to resolve unqualified procedure names that are specified as host variables in SQL CALL statements (CALL host-variable).

## CURRENT PRECISION
Specifies the rules to be used when both operands in a decimal operation have precisions of 15 or less.

## CURRENT QUERY ACCELERATION
Specifies a value that identifies when DB2 sends dynamic SQL queries to an accelerator server and what DB2 does if the accelerator server fails. The special register does not apply to static SQL

queries.

### CURRENT REFRESH AGE
Specifies a timestamp duration value. This duration is the maximum duration since a REFRESH TABLE statement has been processed on a system-maintained REFRESH DEFERRED materialized query table such that the materialized query table can be used to optimize the processing of a query. This special register affects dynamic statement cache matching.

### CURRENT ROUTINE VERSION
Specifies the version identifier that is to be used when invoking a native SQL procedure. CURRENT ROUTINE VERSION is used for CALL statements that use a host variable to specify the procedure name.

### CURRENT RULES
Specifies whether certain SQL statements are executed in accordance with DB2 rules or the rules of the SQL standard.

### CURRENT SCHEMA
Specifies the schema name used to qualify unqualified database object references in dynamically prepared SQL statements.

### CURRENT SERVER
Specifies the location name of the current server.

### CURRENT SQLID
Specifies the SQL authorization ID of the process.

### CURRENT TEMPORAL BUSINESS_TIME
Specifies a TIMESTAMP(12) value that is used in the default BUSINESS_TIME period specification for references to application-period temporal tables.

### CURRENT TEMPORAL SYSTEM_TIME
Specifies a TIMESTAMP(12) value that is used in the default SYSTEM_TIME period specification for references to system-period temporal tables.

### CURRENT TIME
Specifies a time that is based on a reading of the time-of-day clock when the SQL statement is executed at the current server.

### CURRENT TIMESTAMP
Specifies a timestamp that is based on a reading of the time-of-day clock when the SQL statement is executed at the current server.

### CURRENT TIME ZONE
Specifies a value that contains the difference between UTC and local time as defined by the current server, if the SESSION TIME ZONE special register has not been set.

**ENCRYPTION PASSWORD**
Specifies the encryption password and the password hint (if one exists) that are used by the encryption and decryption built-in functions.

**SESSION_USER**
Specifies the primary authorization ID of the process.

**SESSION TIME ZONE**
Specifies a value that identifies the time zone of the application process.

**USER**
Specifies the primary authorization ID of the process. Same as SESSION_USER.

**NOTE:** You can use all special registers in a user-defined function or a stored procedure. However, you can modify only some of the special registers. The following are the special registers that can be modified:

CURRENT APPLICATION COMPATIBILITY
CURRENT APPLICATION ENCODING SCHEME
CURRENT DEBUG MODE
CURRENT DECFLOAT ROUNDING MODE
CURRENT DEGREE
CURRENT EXPLAIN MODE
CURRENT GET_ACCEL_ARCHIVE
CURRENT LOCALE LC_CTYPE
CURRENT MAINTAINED TABLE TYPES FOR OPTIMIZATION
CURRENT OPTIMIZATION HINT
CURRENT PACKAGE PATH
CURRENT PACKAGESET
CURRENT PATH
CURRENT PRECISION
CURRENT QUERY ACCELERATION
CURRENT REFRESH AGE
CURRENT ROUTINE VERSION
CURRENT RULES
CURRENT SCHEMA
CURRENT SQLID1
CURRENT TEMPORAL BUSINESS_TIME
CURRENT TEMPORAL SYSTEM_TIME
ENCRYPTION PASSWORD

# BUILT-IN FUNCTIONS

Built-in functions can be used in SQL statements to return a result based on an argument. These functions are great productivity tools because they can replace custom coded functionality in an application program. Whether your role is application developer, DBA or business services professional, the DB2 built-in functions can save you a great deal of time and effort if you know what they are and how to use them.

There are three types of builtin functions:

1. Aggregate
2. Scalar
3. Table

We'll look at examples of each of these.

## AGGREGATE Functions

An aggregate function receives a set of values for each argument (such as the values of a column) and returns a single-value result for the set of input values. These are especially useful in data analytics. Here are some examples of commonly used aggregate functions.

## AVERAGE

The average function returns the average of a set of numbers. Using our EMP_PAY table, you could get the average REGULAR_PAY for your employees like this:

```
SELECT AVG(EMP_REGULAR_PAY)
FROM EMP_PAY;
---------+---------+---------+---------+--

---------+---------+---------+---------+--
     75000.00000000000000000000000
DSNE610I NUMBER OF ROWS DISPLAYED IS 1
```

## COUNT

The COUNT function returns the number of rows or values in a set of rows or values. Suppose you want to know how many employees you have. You could use this SQL to find out:

```
SELECT COUNT(*)
FROM EMPLOYEE;
---------+---------+---------+---------+-----

          8
DSNE610I NUMBER OF ROWS DISPLAYED IS 1
```

## MAX

The MAX function returns the maximum value in a set of values.

## MIN

The MIN function returns the minimum value in a set of values.

In the next two examples, we use the MAX and MIN functions to determine the highest and lowest paid employees:

```
SELECT MAX(EMP_REGULAR_PAY)
FROM EMP_PAY;
---------+---------+--------

---------+---------+--------
  85000.00
```

Now if we want know which both the maximum salary and the employee who earns it, it is a bit more complex, but not much:

```
SELECT EMP_ID, EMP_REGULAR_PAY
FROM EMP_PAY
WHERE EMP_REGULAR_PAY =
(SELECT MAX(EMP_REGULAR_PAY) FROM EMP_PAY)
;
---------+---------+---------+---------+------
    EMP_ID   EMP_REGULAR_PAY
---------+---------+---------+---------+------
      7459         85000.00
```

Similarly, we can find the minimum using the MIN function.

```
SELECT MIN(EMP_REGULAR_PAY)
FROM EMP_PAY;
---------+---------+---------+-

---------+---------+---------+-
  65000.00

SELECT EMP_ID, EMP_REGULAR_PAY
FROM EMP_PAY
WHERE EMP_REGULAR_PAY =
(SELECT MIN(EMP_REGULAR_PAY) FROM EMP_PAY);
---------+---------+---------+---------+---
    EMP_ID   EMP_REGULAR_PAY
---------+---------+---------+---------+---
      3217         65000.00
```

## SUM

The SUM function returns the sum of a set of numbers. Suppose you need to know what your base payroll will be for the year. You could find out with this SQL:

```
SELECT SUM(EMP_REGULAR_PAY)
FROM EMP_PAY;
---------+---------+---------+---------

---------+---------+---------+---------
        375000.00
DSNE610I NUMBER OF ROWS DISPLAYED IS 1
```

## SCALAR Functions

A scalar function can be used wherever an expression can be used. It is often used to calculate a value or to influence the result of a query. Again we'll provide some examples.

## COALESCE

The COALESCE function returns the value of the first nonnull expression. It is normally used to assign some alternate value when a NULL value is encountered that would otherwise cause an entire record to be excluded from the results. For example, consider the EMP_PAY table with data as follows:

```
SELECT *
FROM EMP_PAY;
---------+---------+---------+---------+---------
   EMP_ID  EMP_REGULAR_PAY  EMP_BONUS_PAY
---------+---------+---------+---------+---------
     3217         65000.00         5500.00
     7459         85000.00         4500.00
     9134         75000.00         2500.00
     4720         80000.00         2500.00
     6288         70000.00         2000.00
DSNE610I NUMBER OF ROWS DISPLAYED IS 5
```

To demonstrate how COALESCE works, let's change the bonus pay amount for employee 9134 to NULL.

```
UPDATE HRSCHEMA.EMP_PAY
SET EMP_BONUS_PAY = NULL
WHERE EMP_ID = 9134;
```

Now our data looks like this:

```
SELECT * FROM HRSCHEMA.EMP_PAY;
---------+---------+---------+---------+------
   EMP_ID  EMP_REGULAR_PAY  EMP_BONUS_PAY
---------+---------+---------+---------+------
     3217         65000.00         5500.00
     7459         85000.00         4500.00
     9134         75000.00      -------------
     4720         80000.00         2500.00
     6288         70000.00         2000.00
DSNE610I NUMBER OF ROWS DISPLAYED IS 5
```

Ok, here's the example. Let's find the average bonus pay in the EMP_PAY table.

```
SELECT AVG(EMP_BONUS_PAY)
AS AVERAGE_BONUS
```

```
   FROM EMP_PAY;
---------+---------+---------+---------
                    AVERAGE_BONUS
---------+---------+---------+---------
      3625.000000000000000000000
```

There is a potential problem here! The problem is that the average bonus is not 3625, it is 2900 (total 14,500 divided by five employees). The problem here is that one of the employee records has NULL in the EMP_BONUS_PAY column. Consequently this record was excluded from the calculated average because NULL is not a numeric value and therefore cannot be included in a computation.

Assuming that you do want to include this record in your results to get the correct average, you will need to convert the NULL to numeric value zero. You can do this using the COALESCE function.

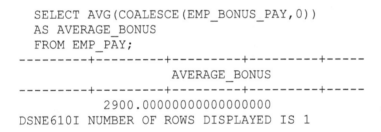

```
   SELECT AVG(COALESCE(EMP_BONUS_PAY,0))
   AS AVERAGE_BONUS
   FROM EMP_PAY;
---------+---------+---------+---------+-----
                    AVERAGE_BONUS
---------+---------+---------+---------+-----
         2900.00000000000000000
DSNE610I NUMBER OF ROWS DISPLAYED IS 1
```

The above says calculate the average EMP_BONUS_PAY using the first non-null value of EMP_BONUS_PAY or zero. Since employee 9134 has a NULL value in the EMP_BONUS_PAY field, the COALESCE function substitutes a zero instead of the NULL. Zero is a numeric value, so this record can now be included in the computation of the average. This gives the correct average which is 2900.

Before we move on let's reset the bonus pay on our employee 9134 so that it can be used correctly for other queries later in the study guide.

```
UPDATE HRSCHEMA.EMP_PAY
SET EMP_BONUS_PAY = 2500.00
WHERE EMP_ID = 9134;
```

You can use COALESCE anytime you need to include a record that would otherwise be excluded due to a NULL value. Converting the NULL to a value will ensure the record can be included in the results.

## CONCAT

The CONCAT function combines two or more strings. Suppose for example you want to list each employee's first and last names from the EMPLOYEE table. You could so it with this SQL:

```
SELECT
CONCAT(CONCAT(EMP_FIRST_NAME,' '),EMP_LAST_NAME)
AS EMP_FULL_NAME
FROM HRSCHEMA.EMPLOYEE;
---------+---------+---------+---------+---------+---
EMP_FULL_NAME
---------+---------+---------+---------+---------+---
EDWARD JOHNSON
BETTY STEWART
BRIANNA FRANKLIN
FRED TURNBULL
TIM SCHULTZ
JOE WILLARD
JAMEs FORD
ELISA HARRIS
DSNE610I NUMBER OF ROWS DISPLAYED IS 8
```

## LCASE

The LCASE function returns a string in which all the characters are converted to lowercase characters. I can't think of many good applications for this, but here is an example of formatting the last name of each employee to lower case. Note: this function does not change any value on the table, it is only formatting the value for presentation.

```
SELECT EMP_ID, LCASE(EMP_LAST_NAME)
FROM HRSCHEMA.EMPLOYEE;
---------+---------+---------+---------+---
    EMP_ID
---------+---------+---------+---------+---
      3217  johnson
      7459  stewart
      9134  franklin
      4175  turnbull
      4720  schultz
      6288  willard
      3333  ford
      7777  harris
DSNE610I NUMBER OF ROWS DISPLAYED IS 8
```

## LEFT

The LEFT function returns a string that consists of the specified number of leftmost bytes of the specified string units. Suppose you have an application that needs the first four letters of the last name (my pharmacy does this as part of the automated prescription filling process). You could accomplish that with this SQL:

```
   SELECT EMP_ID, LEFT(EMP_LAST_NAME,4)
   FROM HRSCHEMA.EMPLOYEE;
---------+---------+---------+---------+-----
    EMP_ID
---------+---------+---------+---------+-----
      3217   JOHN
      7459   STEW
      9134   FRAN
      4175   TURN
      4720   SCHU
      6288   WILL
      3333   FORD
      7777   HARR
DSNE610I NUMBER OF ROWS DISPLAYED IS 8
```

## MAX

The MAX function returns the maximum value in a set of values. For example if we wanted to know the largest base pay for our EMP_PAY table, we could use this SQL:

```
SELECT MAX(EMP_REGULAR_PAY)
AS HIGHEST_PAY
FROM HRSCHEMA.EMP_PAY;
---------+---------+-------
HIGHEST_PAY
---------+---------+-------
   85000.00
```

## MIN

The MIN scalar function returns the minimum value in a set of values. For example if we wanted to know the largest base pay for our EMP_PAY table, we could use this SQL:

```
SELECT MIN(EMP_REGULAR_PAY)
AS LOWEST_PAY
FROM HRSCHEMA.EMP_PAY

---------+---------+-------
LOWEST_PAY
---------+---------+-------
   65000.00
```

## MONTH

The MONTH function returns the month part of a date value. We used this one earlier to compare the month of the employee's promotion to the current month.

94

```
SELECT
EMP_ID,
EMP_PROMOTION_DATE,
CURRENT DATE AS RQST_DATE
FROM HRSCHEMA.EMPLOYEE
WHERE MONTH(EMP_PROMOTION_DATE)
 = MONTH(CURRENT DATE);


---------+---------+---------+---------+---------+----
     EMP_ID  EMP_PROMOTION_DATE  RQST_DATE
---------+---------+---------+---------+---------+----
       3217  2017-01-01          2017-01-19
       7459  2016-01-01          2017-01-19
       4720  2017-01-01          2017-01-19
       6288  2016-01-01          2017-01-19
DSNE610I NUMBER OF ROWS DISPLAYED IS 4
```

## REPEAT

The REPEAT function returns a character string that is composed of an argument that is repeated a specified number of times. Suppose for example that you wanted to display 10 asterisks as a literal field on a report. You could specify it this way:

```
SELECT
EMP_ID,
REPEAT('*',10) AS "FILLER LITERAL",
EMP_SERVICE_YEARS
FROM HRSCHEMA.EMPLOYEE;


---------+---------+---------+---------+---------+-
     EMP_ID  FILLER LITERAL  EMP_SERVICE_YEARS
---------+---------+---------+---------+---------+-
       3217  **********                       6
       7459  **********                       7
       9134  **********                       0
       4175  **********                       1
       4720  **********                       9
       6288  **********                       6
       3333  **********                       7
       7777  **********                       2
DSNE610I NUMBER OF ROWS DISPLAYED IS 8
```

## SPACE

The SPACE function returns a character string that consists of the number of blanks that the argument specifies. You could use this in place of the quotation literals (especially when you want a lot of spaces). The example I'll give uses the SPACE function instead of having to concatenate an empty string using quotation marks.

```
SELECT
CONCAT(CONCAT(EMP_FIRST_NAME,SPACE(1)),
EMP_LAST_NAME)
AS EMP_FULL_NAME
FROM HRSCHEMA.EMPLOYEE;


---------+---------+---------+---------+----
EMP_FULL_NAME
---------+---------+---------+---------+----
EDWARD JOHNSON
BETTY STEWART
BRIANNA FRANKLIN
FRED TURNBULL
TIM SCHULTZ
JOE WILLARD
JAMEs FORD
ELISA HARRIS
DSNE610I NUMBER OF ROWS DISPLAYED IS 8
```

## SUBSTR

The SUBSTR function returns a substring of a string. Let's use the earlier example of retrieving the first four letters of the last name via the LEFT function. You could also accomplish that with this SQL:

```
SELECT EMP_ID, SUBSTR(EMP_LAST_NAME,1,4)
FROM HRSCHEMA.EMPLOYEE;
---------+---------+---------+---------+---
    EMP_ID
---------+---------+---------+---------+---
     3217  JOHN
     7459  STEW
     9134  FRAN
     4175  TURN
     4720  SCHU
     6288  WILL
     3333  FORD
     7777  HARR
DSNE610I NUMBER OF ROWS DISPLAYED IS 8
```

The 1,4 means starting in position one for a length of four. Of course, you could use a different starting position. An example that might make more sense is reformatting the current date. For example:

```
SELECT CURRENT DATE,
SUBSTR(CHAR(CURRENT DATE),6,2)
|| '/'
||SUBSTR(CHAR(CURRENT DATE),9,2)
|| '/'
|| SUBSTR(CHAR(CURRENT DATE),1,4)
```

```
AS REFORMED_DATE
FROM SYSIBM.SYSDUMMY1;
---------+---------+---------+---
             REFORMED_DATE
---------+---------+---------+---
2017-01-12  01/12/2017
```

## UCASE

The UCASE function returns a string in which all the characters are converted to uppercase characters. Here is an example of changing the last name of each employee to upper case. First we will have to covert the uppercase EMP_LAST_NAME values to lowercase. We can do that using the LOWER function. Let's do this for a single row:

```
UPDATE HRSCHEMA.EMPLOYEE
SET EMP_LAST_NAME
= LOWER(EMP_LAST_NAME)
WHERE EMP_ID = 3217;
```

We can verify that the data did in fact get changed to lower case.

```
SELECT EMP_LAST_NAME
FROM HRSCHEMA.EMPLOYEE
WHERE EMP_ID = 3217;
---------+---------+---------+---------
EMP_LAST_NAME
---------+---------+---------+---------
johnson
DSNE610I NUMBER OF ROWS DISPLAYED IS 1
```

Now let's use the UCASE function to have the EMP_LAST_NAME display as upper case.

```
  SELECT EMP_ID, UCASE(EMP_LAST_NAME)
  FROM HRSCHEMA.EMPLOYEE
  WHERE EMP_ID = 3217;
---------+---------+---------+---------+---------
    EMP_ID
---------+---------+---------+---------+---------
      3217  JOHNSON
DSNE610I NUMBER OF ROWS DISPLAYED IS 1
```

Note that the SELECT query did not change any data on the table. We have simply reformatted the data for presentation. Now let's actually convert the data on the record back to upper case:

```
UPDATE HRSCHEMA.EMPLOYEE
SET EMP_LAST_NAME = UPPER(EMP_LAST_NAME)
WHERE EMP_ID = 3217;
```

And we'll verify that it reverted back to uppercase:

```
SELECT EMP_LAST_NAME
FROM HRSCHEMA.EMPLOYEE
WHERE EMP_ID = 3217;
---------+---------+---------+---------+---
EMP_LAST_NAME
---------+---------+---------+---------+---
JOHNSON
DSNE610I NUMBER OF ROWS DISPLAYED IS 1
```

## YEAR

The YEAR function returns the year part of a value that is a character or graphic string. The value must be a valid string representation of a date or timestamp.

```
SELECT CURRENT DATE AS TODAYS_DATE,
YEAR(CURRENT DATE) AS CURRENT_YEAR
FROM SYSIBM.SYSDUMMY1;

---------+---------+---------+--------
TODAYS_DATE   CURRENT_YEAR
---------+---------+---------+--------
2017-01-12             2017
```

## TABLE Functions

These functions are primarily used by system administrators and/or DBAs. It is good to know what they do, but it is unlikely that you would be using them for programmer tasks.

**ADMIN_TASK_LIST**
The ADMIN_TASK_LIST function returns a table with one row for each of the tasks that are defined in the administrative task scheduler task list.

**ADMIN_TASK_OUTPUT**
For an execution of a stored procedure, the ADMIN_TASK_OUTPUT function returns the output parameter values and result sets, if available. If the task that was executed is not a stored procedure or the requested execution status is not available, the function returns an empty table.

**ADMIN_TASK_STATUS**
The ADMIN_TASK_STATUS function returns a table with one row for each task that is defined in the administrative task scheduler task list. Each row indicates the status of the task for the last time it was run.

**MQREADALL**
The MQREADALL function returns a table that contains the messages and message metadata from a specified MQSeries® location without removing the messages from the queue.

**MQREADALLCLOB**

The MQREADALLCLOB function returns a table that contains the messages and message metadata from a specified MQSeries location without removing the messages from the queue.

**MQRECEIVEALL**

The MQRECEIVEALL function returns a table that contains the messages and message metadata from a specified MQSeries location and removes the messages from the queue.

**MQRECEIVEALLCLOB**

The MQRECEIVEALLCLOB function returns a table that contains the messages and message metadata from a specified MQSeries location and removes the messages from the queue.

**XMLTABLE**

The XMLTABLE function returns a result table from the evaluation of XQuery expressions, possibly by using specified input arguments as XQuery variables. Each item in the result sequence of the row XQuery expression represents one row of the result table.

# ROW functions

**UNPACK**

The UNPACK function returns a row of values that are derived from unpacking the input binary string. It is used to unpack a string that was encoded according to the PACK function.

100

# CURSORS

A cursor is a pointer to a record in a result set returned in an application program or stored procedure. If you do programming in DB2 with result sets, you will need to understand cursors. First let's talk about the types of cursors and the rules governing them. That will give you a good idea of what type of cursor to select for your processing. Then we'll provide a programming example of using a cursor.

## Types of Cursors

Cursors are scrollable or nonscrollable, sensitive or insensitive, static or dynamic. A non-scrollable cursor moves sequentially through a result set. A scrollable cursor can move where you want it to move within the result set. Scrollable cursors can be sensitive or insensitive. A sensitive cursor can be static or dynamic.

To declare a cursor as scrollable, you use the SCROLL keyword. In addition, a scrollable cursor is either sensitive or insensitive, and you specify this with the SENSITIVE and INSENSITIVE keywords. Finally to specify a sensitive cursors as static or dynamic, use the STATIC or DYNAMIC keyword.

### INSENSITIVE SCROLL

If you declare a cursor as INSENSITIVE SCROLL, it means that the result set is static. Neither the size nor the ordering of the rows can be changed. Also you cannot change any data values of the rows. Finally, if any rows change in the underlying table or view after you open the cursor, those changes will not be visible to the cursor (and the changes will not be reflected in the result set).

### SENSITIVE STATIC SCROLL

If you declare a cursor as SENSITIVE STATIC SCROLL, it means that the result set is static. Neither the size nor the ordering of the rows can be changed. If any rows change in the underlying table or view after you open the cursor, those changes will not be visible to the cursor (and the changes will not be reflected in the result set). An exception to this is if you specify SENSITIVE on the FETCH statement

You **can** change the rows in the rowset and the changes will be reflected in the result set. Also, if you change a row such that it no longer satisfies the query upon which the cursor is based, that row disappears from the result set. Additionally, if a row in a result set is deleted from the underlying table, the row will disappear from the result set.

### SENSITIVE DYNAMIC SCROLL

If you declare a cursor as SENSITIVE DYNAMIC SCROLL, it means that the size of the result set and the ordering can change each time you do a fetch. The rowset would change if there are any changes to the underlying table after the cursor is opened.

Any rows in the rowset can be changed and deleted, and the changes will be reflected in the result set. If you change a row such that it no longer satisfies the query upon which the cursor is based, that row disappears from the result set. Additionally, if a row in a result set is deleted from the underlying table, the row will disappear from the result set.

## Additional Cursor Options

A cursor can specify WITHOUT HOLD or WITH HOLD, the main difference being whether or not the cursor is closed on a COMMIT. Specifying WITHOUT HOLD allows a cursor to be closed when a COMMIT operation occurs. Specifying WITH HOLD prevents the cursor from being closed when a COMMIT takes place.

A cursor can specify WITHOUT RETURN or WITH RETURN, the difference being whether the result set is intended to be returned to a calling program or procedure. Specifying WITH RETURN means that the result set is meant to be returned from the procedure it is generated in. Specifying WITHOUT RETURN means that the cursor's result set is not intended to be returned from the procedure it is generated in.

A cursor can also specify WITH ROWSET POSITIONING or WITHOUT ROWSET POSITIONING. If you specify WITH ROWSET POSITIONING, then your cursor can return either a single row or rowset (multiple rows) with a single FETCH statement. If WITHOUT ROWSET POSITIONING is specified, it means the cursor can only return a single row with a FETCH statement.

## Sample Program

To use cursors in a program, you must:

1. Declare the cursor

2. Open the Cursor

3. Fetch the cursor (one or more times)

4. Close the cursor

I suggest you memorize the sequence above.

Here is a basic program that uses a cursor to retrieve and update records. We showed this same program earlier to demonstrate the positioned UPDATE operation. If you haven't used cursors much, I suggest getting very familiar with the structure of this program.

Let's say that we want to check all records in the EMPLOYEE table and if the last name is in lower case, we want to change it to upper case and display the employee number of the corrected record. Let's first set up some test data:

```
UPDATE HRSCHEMA.EMPLOYEE
SET EMP_LAST_NAME = LOWER(EMP_LAST_NAME)
WHERE
EMP_LAST_NAME IN ('JOHNSON', 'STEWART', 'FRANKLIN');
```

After you execute this SQL, here's the current content of the EMPLOYEE table:

```
  SELECT EMP_ID, EMP_LAST_NAME, EMP_FIRST_NAME
  FROM HRSCHEMA.EMPLOYEE;
---------+---------+---------+---------+---------+-----
    EMP_ID  EMP_LAST_NAME          EMP_FIRST_NAME
---------+---------+---------+---------+---------+-----
      3217  johnson                EDWARD
      7459  stewart                BETTY
      9134  franklin               BRIANNA
      4720  SCHULTZ                TIM
      6288  WILLARD                JOE
      1122  JENKINS                DEBBIE
      4175  TURNBULL               FREDERICK
      1001  HENDERSON              JOHN
DSNE610I NUMBER OF ROWS DISPLAYED IS 8
```

To accomplish our objective we'll define and open a cursor on the EMPLOYEE table. We can specify a WHERE clause that limits the result set to only those records that contain lower case characters. After we find them, we will change the case to upper and replace the records.

First we need to identify the rows that include lower case letters in column EMP_LAST_NAME. We can do this using the UPPER function. We'll compare the current contents of the EMP_LAST_NAME to the value of UPPER(EMP_LAST_NAME) and if the results are not identical, the row in question has lower case and needs to be changed. Our result set should include all rows where these two values are not identical. So our SQL would be:

```
SELECT EMP_ID, EMP_LAST_NAME
FROM EMPLOYEE
WHERE EMP_LAST_NAME <> UPPER(EMP_LAST_NAME)
```

Once we've placed the last name value in the host variable EMP-LAST-NAME, we can use the COBOL Upper-case function to convert lowercase to uppercase.

```
MOVE FUNCTION UPPER-CASE (EMP-LAST-NAME) TO EMP-LAST-NAME
```

Now we are ready to write the program. Actually we presented this same program earlier when demonstrating the UPDATE function. Since we are focused on the cursor part of it this time, let's review.

We define and open the cursor, cycle through the result set using FETCH, modify the data and then do the UPDATE action specifying the current record of the cursor. That is what is meant by a positioned update – the cursor is positioned on the record to be changed, hence you do not need to specify a more elaborate WHERE clause in the UPDATE. Only the WHERE **CURRENT OF <cursor name>** clause need be specified. Also we will include the **FOR UPDATE** clause in our cursor definition to ensure DB2 knows our intent is to update the data we retrieve.

The program code follows:

```
        IDENTIFICATION DIVISION.
        PROGRAM-ID. COBEMP2.


        **********************************************************
        *        PROGRAM USING DB2 CURSOR HANDLING             *
        **********************************************************

        ENVIRONMENT DIVISION.
        DATA DIVISION.
        WORKING-STORAGE SECTION.

            EXEC SQL
               INCLUDE SQLCA
            END-EXEC.


            EXEC SQL
               INCLUDE EMPLOYEE
            END-EXEC.

            EXEC SQL
                DECLARE EMP-CURSOR CURSOR FOR
                SELECT EMP_ID, EMP_LAST_NAME
                FROM EMPLOYEE
                WHERE EMP_LAST_NAME <> UPPER(EMP_LAST_NAME)
                FOR UPDATE OF EMP_LAST_NAME
            END-EXEC.


        PROCEDURE DIVISION.

        MAIN-PARA.
            DISPLAY "SAMPLE COBOL PROGRAM: UPDATE USING CURSOR".
```

```
      EXEC SQL
          OPEN EMP-CURSOR
      END-EXEC.

      DISPLAY 'OPEN CURSOR SQLCODE: ' SQLCODE.

      PERFORM FETCH-CURSOR
        UNTIL SQLCODE NOT EQUAL 0.

      EXEC SQL
          CLOSE EMP-CURSOR
      END-EXEC.

      DISPLAY 'CLOSE CURSOR SQLCODE: ' SQLCODE.

      STOP RUN.

   FETCH-CURSOR.

      EXEC SQL
          FETCH EMP-CURSOR INTO :EMP-ID, :EMP-LAST-NAME
      END-EXEC.

      IF SQLCODE = 0
         DISPLAY 'BEFORE CHANGE  ', EMP-LAST-NAME
         MOVE FUNCTION UPPER-CASE (EMP-LAST-NAME)
           TO EMP-LAST-NAME
         EXEC SQL
           UPDATE EMPLOYEE
           SET EMP_LAST_NAME = :EMP-LAST-NAME
           WHERE CURRENT OF EMP-CURSOR
         END-EXEC

      END-IF.

      IF SQLCODE = 0
         DISPLAY 'AFTER CHANGE   ', EMP-LAST-NAME
      END-IF.
```

Here is the output from running the program:

```
SAMPLE COBOL PROGRAM: UPDATE USING CURSOR
OPEN CURSOR SQLCODE: 0000000000
BEFORE CHANGE   johnson
AFTER CHANGE    JOHNSON
BEFORE CHANGE   stewart
AFTER CHANGE    STEWART
BEFORE CHANGE   franklin
AFTER CHANGE    FRANKLIN
CLOSE CURSOR SQLCODE: 0000000000
```

Here is the PLI version of the program.

```
PLIEMP2: PROCEDURE OPTIONS(MAIN) REORDER;

 /******************************************************************
 * PROGRAM NAME :   PLIEMP2 - USE CURSOR TO UPDATE DB2 ROWS        *
 ******************************************************************/

 /******************************************************************
 /*                W O R K I N G   S T O R A G E                  *
 ******************************************************************/


    DCL RET_SQL_CODE              FIXED BIN(31) INIT(0);
    DCL RET_SQL_CODE_PIC          PIC 'S999999999' INIT (0);


    EXEC SQL
      INCLUDE SQLCA;

    EXEC SQL
      INCLUDE EMPLOYEE;

    EXEC SQL
      DECLARE EMP_CURSOR CURSOR FOR
      SELECT EMP_ID, EMP_LAST_NAME
      FROM HRSCHEMA.EMPLOYEE
      WHERE EMP_LAST_NAME <> UPPER(EMP_LAST_NAME)
      FOR UPDATE OF EMP_LAST_NAME;

 /******************************************************************
 /*                P R O G R A M   M A I N L I N E               *
 ******************************************************************/

    PUT SKIP LIST ('SAMPLE PLI PROGRAM: CURSOR TO UPDATE ROWS');

    EXEC SQL OPEN EMP_CURSOR;

    PUT SKIP LIST ('OPEN CURSOR SQLCODE: ' || SQLCODE);

    IF SQLCODE = 0 THEN
       DO UNTIL (SQLCODE ¬= 0);
          CALL P0100_FETCH_CURSOR;
       END;

    EXEC SQL CLOSE EMP_CURSOR;

    PUT SKIP LIST ('CLOSE CURSOR SQLCODE: ' || SQLCODE);
```

```
    IF SQLCODE ¬= 0 THEN
       DO;
          EXEC SQL
             GET DIAGNOSTICS CONDITION 1
                :RET_SQL_CODE  = DB2_RETURNED_SQLCODE;

          RET_SQL_CODE_PIC  = RET_SQL_CODE;
          PUT SKIP LIST (RET_SQL_CODE_PIC);
       END;

 P0100_FETCH_CURSOR: PROC;

    EXEC SQL
        FETCH EMP_CURSOR INTO :EMP_ID, :EMP_LAST_NAME;

    IF SQLCODE = 0 THEN
       DO;
          PUT SKIP LIST ('BEFORE CHANGE  ' || EMP_LAST_NAME);
          EMP_LAST_NAME = UPPERCASE(EMP_LAST_NAME);
          EXEC SQL
             UPDATE HRSCHEMA.EMPLOYEE
             SET EMP_LAST_NAME = :EMP_LAST_NAME
             WHERE CURRENT OF EMP_CURSOR;
          IF SQLCODE = 0 THEN
             PUT SKIP LIST ('AFTER CHANGE  ' || EMP_LAST_NAME);
       END;

END P0100_FETCH_CURSOR;

END PLIEMP2;
```

And here is the modified table:

```
  SELECT EMP_ID,
  EMP_LAST_NAME,
  EMP_FIRST_NAME
  FROM HRSCHEMA.EMPLOYEE;
---------+---------+---------+---------+---------+-----
    EMP_ID  EMP_LAST_NAME        EMP_FIRST_NAME
---------+---------+---------+---------+---------+-----
      3217  JOHNSON              EDWARD
      7459  STEWART              BETTY
      9134  FRANKLIN             BRIANNA
      4720  SCHULTZ              TIM
      6288  WILLARD              JOE
      1122  JENKINS              DEBBIE
      4175  TURNBULL             FREDERICK
      1001  HENDERSON            JOHN
DSNE610I NUMBER OF ROWS DISPLAYED IS 8
```

This method of using a positioned cursor update is something you will use often, particularly when you do not know your result set beforehand, or anytime you need to examine the content of the record before you perform the update.

# SQLCODES
## Common Error SQLCODES
These are the more common SQL error codes you may receive and their meaning.

-117     THE NUMBER OF VALUES ASSIGNED IS NOT THE SAME AS THE NUMBER OF SPECIFIED OR IMPLIED COLUMNS

-180     THE DATE, TIME, OR TIMESTAMP VALUE value IS INVALID

-181     THE STRING REPRESENTATION OF A DATETIME VALUE IS NOT A VALID DATETIME VALUE

-203     A REFERENCE TO COLUMN column-name IS AMBIGUOUS

-206     Object-name IS NOT VALID IN THE CONTEXT WHERE IT IS USED

-305     THE NULL VALUE CANNOT BE ASSIGNED TO OUTPUT HOST VARIABLE NUMBER position-number BECAUSE NO INDICATOR VARIABLE IS SPECIFIED

-501     THE CURSOR IDENTIFIED IN A FETCH OR CLOSE STATEMENT IS NOT OPEN

-502     THE CURSOR IDENTIFIED IN AN OPEN STATEMENT IS ALREADY OPEN

-803     AN INSERTED OR UPDATED VALUE IS INVALID BECAUSE THE INDEX IN INDEX SPACE indexspace-name CONSTRAINS COLUMNS OF THE TABLE SO NO TWO ROWS CAN CONTAIN DUPLICATE VALUES IN THOSE COLUMNS. RID OF EXISTING ROW IS X record-id

-805     DBRM OR PACKAGE NAME location-name.collection-id.dbrm-name.consistency-token NOT FOUND IN PLAN plan-name. REASON reason-code

-811     THE RESULT OF AN EMBEDDED SELECT STATEMENT OR A SUBSELECT IN THE SET CLAUSE OF AN UPDATE STATEMENT IS A TABLE OF MORE THAN ONE ROW, OR THE RESULT OF A SUBQUERY OF A BASIC PREDICATE IS MORE THAN ONE VALUE

-818     THE PRECOMPILER-GENERATED TIMESTAMP x IN THE LOAD MODULE IS DIFFERENT FROM THE BIND TIMESTAMP y BUILT FROM THE DBRM z

-904     UNSUCCESSFUL EXECUTION CAUSED BY AN UNAVAILABLE RESOURCE. REASON reason-code, TYPE OF RESOURCE resource-type, AND RESOURCE NAME resource-name.

-911     THE CURRENT UNIT OF WORK HAS BEEN ROLLED BACK DUE TO DEADLOCK OR TIMEOUT. REASON reason-code, TYPE OF RESOURCE resource-type, AND RESOURCE NAME resource-name

```
-913     UNSUCCESSFUL EXECUTION CAUSED BY DEADLOCK OR TIMEOUT. REASON
         CODE  reason-code,  TYPE  OF  RESOURCE  resource-type,  AND
         RESOURCE NAME resource-name.

-922     AUTHORIZATION FAILURE: error-type ERROR. REASON reason-code.
```

The complete list of error SQLCODES is available on the IBM Knowledge Center.

# Dynamic versus Static SQL

## Static SQL

Static SQL statements are embedded within an application program that is written in a traditional programming language such as COBOL or PL/I. The statement is prepared before the program is executed, and the executable statement persists after the program ends. You can use static SQL when you know before run time what SQL statements your application needs to use.

As a practical matter, when you use static SQL you cannot change the form of SQL statements unless you make changes to the program and recompile and bind it. However, you can increase the flexibility of those statements by using host variables. So for example you could write an SQL that retrieves employee information for all employees with X years of service where the X becomes a host variable that you load at run time. Using static SQL and host variables is more secure than using dynamic SQL.

## Dynamic SQL

Unlike static SQL which is prepared before the program runs, with dynamic SQL DB2 prepares and executes the SQL statements at run time as part of the program's execution. Dynamic SQL is a good choice when you do not know the format of an SQL statement before you write or run a program. An example might be a user interface that allows a web application to submit SQL statements to a background COBOL program for execution. In this case, you wouldn't know the structure of the statement the client submits until run time.

Applications that use dynamic SQL create an SQL statement in the form of a character string. A typical dynamic SQL application takes the following steps:

1. Translates the input data into an SQL statement.

2. Prepares the SQL statement to execute and acquires a description of the result table (if any).

3. Obtains, for SELECT statements, enough main storage to contain retrieved data.

4. Executes the statement or fetches the rows of data.

5. Processes the returned information.

6. Handles SQL return codes.

## Performance Comparison of Static versus Dynamic SQL

Ordinarily static SQL is more efficient than dynamic because the former is prepared and optimized before the program executes. For static SQL statements DB2 typically determines the access path when you bind the plan or package - the exception being if you code REOPT(ALWAYS) in your bind statement. If you code REOPT(ALWAYS) on a package that has static SQL, DB2 will determine the access path when you bind the plan or package and again at run time using the values of host variables and parameter markers (if included).

For dynamic SQL statements, DB2 determines the access path at run time, when the statement is prepared. The cost of preparing a dynamic statement many times can lead to a performance that is worse than with static SQL. However you can consider these options to improve your performance with dynamic SQL:

1. You can improve performance by caching dynamic statements. To do this, set subsystem parameter CACHEDYN=YES.

2. With dynamic SQL you can also re-optimize your query by using the REOPT bind options. If you are not using the CACHEDYN=YES, you can use the REOPT(ALWAYS) bind option to ensure the best access path. But keep in mind this may slow performance for frequently used dynamic statements.

3. If you are using the CACHEDYN=YES subsystem parameter setting, you can use bind option REOPT(ONCE) and DB2 will only determine the optimal access path the first time the statement is executed. It saves that access path in the dynamic statement cache.

4. If you specify REOPT(AUTO), DB2 will look at any statements with parameter markers and determine whether a new access path might improve performance. If it determines that it would, DB2 will generate a new access path.

To conclude this section, you generally want to use static SQL when you know the structure of your SQL statement and when performance is a significant goal. Use dynamic SQL when you need the flexibility of not knowing the structure of your SQL until run time.

# Next Steps

Congratulations on completing this DB2 SQL basic training! Now that you have the basics completed, let me suggest some next steps.

1. Continue your DB2 training with my DB2 Basic and Intermediate training series:

   **DB2 11.0 for z/OS: Basic Training for Application Developers**

   **DB2 11.0 for z/OS: Intermediate Training for Application Developers**

   More information can be found about these books in the Other Titles by Robert Wingate section of this book – just turn a couple pages ahead.

2. If you feel that this book has helped you, please consider leaving a positive review at the source where you purchased it. I'll really appreciate that!


Best of luck with your DB2 career!

Robert Wingate

# Other Titles by Robert Wingate

**DB2 11 for z/OS: Basic Training for Application Developers**

**ISBN 13: 978-1974190676**

This book will help you learn the basic information and skills you need to develop applications with DB2 11 for z/OS. The instruction, examples and questions/answers in this book are a fast track to becoming productive as quickly as possible. The content is easy to read and digest, well organized and focused on honing real job skills. DB2 11 for z/OS Basic Training for Application Developers is a key step in the direction of mastering DB2 application development so you'll be ready to join a technical team.

# DB2 11 for z/OS: Intermediate Training for Application Developers

**ISBN 13: 978-1974233908**

This book will help you learn the intermediate level information and skills you need to develop applications with DB2 11 for z/OS. The instruction, examples and questions/answers in this book are a fast track to becoming productive as quickly as possible. The content is easy to read and digest, well organized and focused on honing real job skills. DB2 11 for z/OS Intermediate Training for Application Developers is a major step in the direction of mastering DB2 application development so you'll be ready to join and/or lead a technical application team.

## DB2 Exam C2090-320 Preparation Guide

ISBN 13: 978-1544852096

This book will help you pass IBM Exam C2090-320 and become an IBM Certified Database Associate - DB2 11 Fundamentals for z/OS. The instruction, examples and questions/answers in the book offer you a significant advantage by helping you to gauge your readiness for the exam, to better understand the objectives being tested, and to get a broad exposure to the DB2 11 knowledge you'll be tested on. The book is also a fine introduction to DB2 for z/OS!

## DB2 Exam C2090-313 Preparation Guide

ISBN 13: 978-1548463052

This book will help you pass IBM Exam C2090-313 and become an IBM Certified Application Developer - DB2 11 for z/OS. The instruction, examples and questions/answers in the book offer you a significant advantage by helping you to gauge your readiness for the exam, to better understand the objectives being tested, and to get a broad exposure to the DB2 11 knowledge you'll be tested on.

**ISBN-13: 978-1720820710**

This book will teach you the basic information and skills you need to develop applications with COBOL on IBM mainframes running z/OS. The instruction, examples and sample programs in this book are a fast track to becoming productive as quickly using COBOL. The content is easy to read and digest, well organized and focused on honing real job skills.

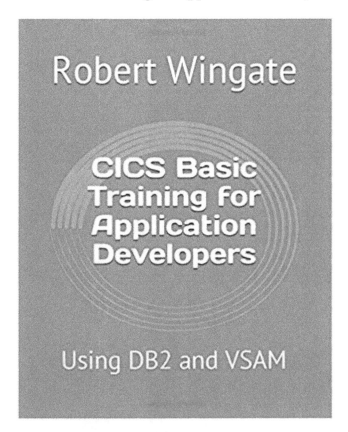

**ISBN-13: 978-1794325067**
This book will teach you the basic information and skills you need to develop applications with CICS on IBM mainframe computers running z/OS. The instruction, examples and sample programs in this book are a fast track to becoming productive as quickly as possible using CICS with the COBOL programming language. The content is easy to read and digest, well organized and focused on honing real job skills.

**IMS Basic Training for Application Developers**

ISBN-13: 978-1793440433

This book will teach you the basic information and skills you need to develop applications with IMS on IBM mainframe computers running z/OS. The instruction, examples and sample programs in this book are a fast track to becoming productive as quickly as possible using IMS with COBOL and PLI. The content is easy to read and digest, well organized and focused on honing real job skills.

**ISBN-13: 978-1986039840**

This book will teach you the basic information and skills you need to develop applications on IBM mainframes running z/OS. The instruction, examples and sample programs in this book are a fast track to becoming productive as quickly as possible in JCL, MVS Utilities, COBOL, PLI and DB2. The content is easy to read and digest, well organized and focused on honing real job skills. IBM z/OS Quick Start Training for Application Developers is a key step in the direction of mastering IBM application development so you'll be ready to join a technical team.

**ISBN-13: 978-1717284594**

This book will teach you the basic information and skills you need to develop applications on IBM mainframes running z/OS. The instruction, examples and sample programs in this book are a fast track to becoming productive as quickly as possible in VSAM, IMS and DB2. The content is easy to read and digest, well organized and focused on honing real job skills. IBM z/OS Quick Start Training for Application Developers is a key step in the direction of mastering IBM application development so you'll be ready to join a technical team.

Additional titles are on the following pages.

## DB2 Exam C2090-313 Practice Questions

ISBN 13: 978-1534992467

This book will help you pass IBM Exam C2090-313 and become an IBM Certified Application Developer - DB2 11 for z/OS. The 180 questions and answers in the book (three full practice exams) offer you a significant advantage by helping you to gauge your readiness for the exam, to better understand the objectives being tested, and to get a broad exposure to the DB2 11 knowledge you'll be tested on.

## DB2 Exam C2090-615 Practice Questions

ISBN 13: 978-1535028349

This book will help you pass IBM Exam C2090-615 and become an IBM Certified Database Associate (DB2 10.5 for Linux, Unix and Windows). The questions and answers in the book offer you a significant advantage by helping you to gauge your readiness for the exam, to better understand the objectives being tested, and to get a broad exposure to the knowledge you'll be tested on.

# About the Author

Robert Wingate is a computer services professional with over 30 years of IBM mainframe programming experience. He holds several IBM certifications, including IBM Certified Application Developer - DB2 11 for z/OS, and IBM Certified Database Administrator for LUW. He lives in Fort Worth, Texas.

# Index

www.ingramcontent.com/pod-product-compliance
Lightning Source LLC
Chambersburg PA
CBHW060154060326
40690CB00018B/4105